Teaching and Inculcating a Healthy Life Style

(Prevention of HIV/AIDS)

- India has had a sharp increase in the estimated number of HIV infections from a few thousand in the early 1990's to a working estimate adults living with HIV/AIDS in 2002 between 3.8 million and 4.6 million.
  — S. Kumar (2003) 'HIV cases rising sharply in India' BMJ, Aug. 2; 327(7409) : 245
- How do you talk about HIV/AIDS to someone who does not know the basics of health and hygiene?
  — The Lancet (2003) 'Spreading the word about HIV/AIDS in India'
  (Ratna Gaekwad, an outreach coordinator with the Delhi NGO Prayatna)

Teaching and Inculcating a Healthy Life Style among Students

(Prevention of HIV/AIDS)

Foreword

Eric Feldman
Professor of Medicine
Well Medical College of Cornell University,
New York

Rajinder M. Kalra
Rakesh Mehta
S. Kalra

SHIPRA

ISBN: 978-81-7541-205-7

2008 Impression
(2005, 2004)

Teaching and Inculcating a Healthy Life Style among Students
(*Prevention of HIV/AIDS*)

Published by:
SHIPRA PUBLICATIONS
115-A, Vikas Marg, Shakarpur
Delhi – 110092 (India)
Ph.: 91-11-65277210, 22500954; Fax: 22458662
Email: info@shiprapublications.com
Website: www.shiprapublications.com

In Loving memory

of

Dr. P.C. Mehta

Mrs. Gargi Devi Kalra

Mr. Amar Nath Kalra

Mrs. Leela Vati Dawar

Their vision helped us to see.

In Loving memory

of

Dr P.C. Mehta

Mrs Gargi Devi Kalra

Mr Amar Nath Kalra

Mrs Leela Vati Dawar

Their vision helped us to see

Foreword

The spread of HIV/AIDS, in third world countries such as India has not been contained. There is a significant role for education in disseminating information about HIV/AIDS. The authors have highlighted the concept of introduction of a healthy life style, based on cultural heritage in India, in school curriculum to prevent an increase in the incidence and prevalence of HIV/AIDS. Since there is no curative, and for many, economically viable treatment thus far, the importance of prevention cannot be overemphasized.

The authors have made sincere and praiseworthy efforts in outlining the role of healthy life styles in preventing HIV/AIDS, with special reference to sex education, which is certainly needed in India where HIV is spreading in epidemic proportions.

The education about healthy life style, through introduction in school curriculum may impart a meaningful change in life style of students who are in a vulnerable phase of their lives. The authors have done an exhaustive review of the role of sex education in various western countries and have attempted to imbibe the lessons learnt from these countries with special emphasis on impact of cultural values and sexual behavior.

The relationship between sex and love has been amply illustrated by the authors such as elucidated by Mahatma Gandhi and the spiritual leader, Krishnamurti.

The concept of teaching about healthy life style in school curriculum is highly recommended. Since the goal of education is to prevent the spread of HIV/AIDS, the health care and teaching institutions should collaborative in this endeavor.

I congratulate the authors for their sincere concern about HIV/AIDS in India.

Eric Feldman
Professor of Medicine
Well Medical College of Cornell University,
New York

Message from Chancellor

International Institute of Adult and Lifelong Education – New Delhi

In a recent publication titled *AIDS - No Time for Complacency*, the World Health Organization warns about the socioeconomic impact of HIV/AIDS: "AIDS threatens the very fabric of society. It affects people in their most productive age, resulting in several direct and indirect economic costs... Because AIDS incapacitates people at ages when they are most needed lor the support of the young and the elderly, the impact on families ... is enormous, and is aggrevated by the frequent stigmatization of people with HIV/AIDS. AIDS will leave millions of children without parents. These AIDS orphans will swell the ranks of street children, already estimated at over 100 million, increasing the number of young people vulnerable to infection with HIV".

WHO estimated that at the end of 2003, there were 37 million adults and 2.5 million children living with HIV that will progressively lead to AIDS. No cure has yet been found for this killer disease nor is likely to be available in the near future. Since AIDS is essentially a sexually transmitted disease, sexual behavior needs to be the prime focus for preventing its transmission. Thus, prevention is indisputably the most important objective of the strategies to combat AIDS.

In any strategy for HIV/AIDS prevention, the need to have an information and education programme aimed at all men and women, including adolescents who are at greater risk of this infection can not be over emphasized. It is in this regard that this publication by Prof. Rajinder Mohan Kalra and his colleagues is very timely. Trapped in the whirlwind of globalization and information technology and the inexorable sway of western life-styles and cultural influences, the adolescents and youth are drifting away from the influence of parents, teachers and elders. And, already under threat of breakdown, the traditional social outlook still disapproves and decries the normal sexual behaviour of the adolescents and youth who seem to be caught up between the appeals of their age and a parental/family, social and cultural milieu that is unable to come to terms with it. At the same time, there is no systematic attempt to provide a comprehensive education package at the school level. Imbuing HIV/AIDS awareness and education in the minds of adolescents who are still in the stage of their education, would equip them with the knowledge and discipline necessary for a life safe from the dreaded disease.

While every country has a national plan and strategies to combat the HIV/AIDS pandemic among children, youth and adults, at least in developing countries like India, there has been no serious attempt to introduce HIV/AIDS awareness at the school level. It is in this regard that this publication is a pioneering attempt to provide a holistic sex education at secondary and senior secondary level. Rather than borrowing the terms in vogue in Western countries like Sex Education or Life Skills, the authors consciously advocate the robust approach of Teaching and Inculcating a Healthy Life Style, an approach that is in harmony with Indian culture, and at the same time includes all the different learning components relating to human biology, sexual behaviour, and awareness about the hazards of un-safe sex life style. We do hope that the approach as well as the contents posited by the authors becomes an integral part of education of the adolescents in India.

K. C. Choudhary

Acknowledgements

The authors express their special thanks to Dr. Eric Feldman for his keen interest in this noble venture and also for writing the Foreword for this book.

Due acknowledgment is made to Dr. Amelia Martinko for being a source of inspiration and moral support to one of the authors, Dr. Mehta.

Needless to say, the authors owe much to numerous humanist educators who have taught them "to Live is to Learn to Love". They include Sai Ram, Reverend Mother Teresa, His Holiness Dalai Lama and late Swami Somanandjee.

The authors express their gratitude to various international organizations (Red Cross Societies, Geneva, WHO, UNDP) and educationists Prof. Kireet Joshi (Chairman, I.C.P.R. Delhi), Prof. Gracious Thomas (AIDS Expert, IGNOU), Dr. M.R. Marathe (AIDS Research Expert, Ranbaxy Pharmaceutical), Mr. K.C. Choudhry (President IIALE), Prof. S.Y. Shah (Vice President IIALE, Delhi) and Sh. J. C. Aggarwal for their encouragement and support. Special thanks is expressed to the following members of the authors' families for providing the inspiration to write this book. They include: Archana / Sanjay Uppal; Nitasha / Piyush Bhatnagar; Anita / Subhash Verma; Bankim, Lalit-Seema Grover; Sonika, Deepali and Shivam Prakash (Mehta); Shreya, Ayushi Uppal and Dheriya, Shourya Grover.

Authors

Preface

The subject of sex, especially in the third world, has been surrounded by myths, superstitions and taboos from time immemorial. Tradition and the moral code in various religions and cultures led to the belief that there is something inherently unholy about sex. With change in life styles, attitudes and media interventions, sex related subjects are being discussed more openly. Co-education, economic needs and quest for freedom and equality have brought out females from behind the guarded walls of their homes. The intermingling of sexes in all spheres of life makes it imperative that we review our values and customs related to sex. Hence, authors in this book have emphasized on fostering of Healthy Life Style among students (India) for prevention of AIDS.

Furthermore, the alarming statistics regarding AIDS/HIV infection (Sexually Transmitted Diseases, in India, and rest of Asia, make it imperative that instructional material on sex education be introduced forthwith in the curricula for secondary and senior secondary education. This is also an accepted fact that introduction of sex education in secondary/senior curriculum will be a Herculean task because of historical, cultural and social perspectives about the concept of sex in the third world. Therefore, in this academic effort, a thrust is on life style rather than sex education which is a component of Life Style Education.

The relevance of sex education as a means of developing healthy personality and attitudes can be advocated on various counts. Sigmund Freud did a valuable service by pointing out that nervous disorders produced in later life could be due to improper teaching of young adolescents matters related to sex.

Adolescents are our future nation builders and it is time to introduce sex education in schools (especially at the secondary and senior secondary levels) in a meaningful manner taking into account cultural, social and moral values.

In this humble academic venture, the authors have made an attempt to suggest a framework to introduce and transact sex education as an integral component or a separate school subject in the secondary school curriculum. The authors' conviction is that introduction of healthy life style education in secondary/senior secondary schools as a co-curricular component may not be of much value. Furthermore, this type of education course or component should be an examinable subject as any other academic subject at the secondary or senior secondary level. In the initial stages and to avoid the problem of curriculum load, it may be incorporated (correlated) in all school subjects at the secondary/senior secondary levels. This may not only be the domain of the biology teachers, but also teachers of all other subjects at the secondary and senior secondary levels.

It is hoped that the framework for introducing healthy life style education in Schools suggested in this book will prove helpful for educational planners and implementers. This book is also suitable for Indo-Canadian and Indo-American students.

Contents

Foreword 7

Message 9

Acknowledments 11

Preface 13

1. Introduction 19

Healthy Life Style – What is it? 19

Healthy Life Style 20

Sex Education; Why the Need is Urgent Now? 21

What is Sex Education? 23

Importance of Sex Education 24

Action Oriented Strategies for Introducing Sex Education 25

2. Sex Education in Schools : An International Perspective 32

What Asia can learn from Europe and Western Hemisphere? 32

Swedish Education Experience – A Unique Achievement 32

Basis of Sex Education in Sweden 34

Sex Education in The United States 36

Sex Education in the United Kingdom (U.K.) 36

Sex Education in Asia 37

Sex Education in Adolescents: Present Scenario 37

Sex and Tradition 39

Conclusion 39

3. Cultural Heritage and Sexual Behaviour 43

Abstinence from Sexual Indulgence 44

Mahatma Gandhi and Sexual Abstinence 44

Sex Sublimating to Spirituality 45

Some Common Beliefs regarding semen 45

Modern Culture and Sexual Abstinence 46

Status of Pre-marital Sex among Adolescents in India 46

Other Sexual Behaviour Patterns in India 48

Male and Female He Created Them 50
Chastity 51
Offences against Chastity 52
Chastity and Homosexuality 54
Teenage Sex : Yes or No 54
Real Love 55
Safe Sex 56
How safe are Contraceptives? 57
Purification of the Heart 58
Contents and Strategies of Sex Education 59

4. Adolescents and AIDS **60**
Basic Information about AIDS 62
Measuring the number of CD4 63
HIV Infection and Illnesses 64
A Few Pointers 65
Females are more AIDS Prone 66
Preventing AIDS through Love/Sex as a Human Value .. 66

5. Inculcation of Human Values amongst Students **69**
Values — Definition 69
Catagories of Values 70
Values in the School System 76
Character Formation and Assessment of Values 77
Does it have to be either Choice? 80
How does one accomplish this task? 80
Real Love 82

6. Curriculum Development and Evaluation in Healthy Life Style Education **85**
Curriculum : What is it? 85
Organisation of a Sex Education Programme 89
Practical Strategies for Developing a Unit 90
Evaluation 91
Evaluation in Sex Education 92

7. Teaching-Learning Strategies **95**
Discussion Method 95
Values Continuum 97

Lecture Method 98
Brain Storming 98
Discovery/Enquiry Method 99
Fill-up the Blank Statements 100
Expert's Advice Column 100
Audio-Visual Aids Method 100
Specialist Speaker 101
Project Method — Case-Study 102
Role Playing 103
Question Cards 103
Popular Songs, Poems (Music) 104

8. Teaching Healthy Life Style 105
Sexual Health – What is it? 105
Sexual Health in Schools 106
Physical/Emotional Changes in Adolescence 106
Talking About Healthy Life Style in Indian Schools 108
Correlation of Sexual Learning with School Subjects 108
Basic Information about STDs 110

9. Integrated Approach to Healthy Life Style Education Instructions 112
Correlation with School Subjects 112
Sex Education and Teaching of Hindi 123
Sex Education and Social Sciences 127

10. Awareness and Involvement of Community (Introducing Healthy Life Style Education in Rural Schools) 128
Role of Community Power Structure 130
Strategies for Change 131
Local Advisory Committee(LAC) 131
Advantages of LAC 132
Purpose of LACs 134
Types of LACs 135
Organization of LACs 136
Selection of the LAC Members. 136
Committee's Membership 137
Qualifications for LAC Members 137

Selection of Officials 138
Suggestions 138
Conclusion 139

11. Meaningful Healthy Life Style Education to the Adolescents : Guidelines for Teachers 141
Compatible Relationships with Students 141
Teacher as a Guide 141
Some Practical Strategies 143
Sex Education – Responsibility of each and every School Teacher 144
Integrated Approach to Teaching and Learning Situation in Sex Education 145
Conclusion 145

Annexures

I Policy Decisions on Health Education in Schools *Education Commission (1964–66)* 146

II India's Recent Programmes to Fight Against HIV/AIDS 164

III Adult HIV Prevalance *Comparative Data of Countries* 169

Suggested Readings 174

Introduction

Healthy Life Style – What is it?

Youngsters especially students today all over the world are a confused lot. They are in the process of breaking away from all that is binding, be it the family, the society or the traditions. Pride in cultural heritage has lost its significance in the shrinking global perimeters. The exposure through the multi-media communications system has widened the generation gap overnight. Adolescents have instantly lapped up with delight whatever has appealed to them and the adults are too 'helpless', too 'slow' to point out the value of rationalization and the dangers of indiscriminately borrowing ideas.

The impact of such rapid changes is felt in every social system, the progressive – conventional or orthodox. But, for a society that has stuck to its past for centuries, such sudden changes can shatter its very fabric. This is what has actually happened to today's youngster in the majority of developing countries such as India. Whereas in the West the social outlook has evolved gradually, in third world countries like India there has been a superficial cultural change – merely grafting of concepts regarding sex, and freedom of expression. In the third world countries, the adolescent today is in the midst of an overwhelming 'values crisis'. The age old customs have lost their relevance and adoption of western values in total is not only impractical but culturally suicidal. What the modern youngster needs is an analytical and rational approach towards life. Only an enlightened older generation of people like parents, teachers and social workers can guide and steer the adolescents to a world that is full of hope, not of dismay and death.

Healthy Life Style

The concept of healthy life style especially relating to sex education has been surrounded by myths, superstitions and taboos from time immemorial. Tradition and the moral code in our religion and culture led to the belief that there is something inherently impure about sex. With the change in life styles and attitudes, sex related subjects are being discussed more openly but the discussions lack a rational or meaningful approach which should be an outcome of a scientific knowledge with reference to their cultural heritage. Co-education, economic needs and quest for freedom have brought out girls from behind the guarded walls of their homes. This intermingling of sexes in all spheres of life makes it imperative that we review our values and customs related to matters of sex. Coming to the specifics of Healthy Life Style and AIDS Prevention, it is worth mentioning that preaching celibacy, abstinence or *brahamcharya* would be the best solution but it may not be very successful as it may be relevant to a limited extent especially in the rural and semi-urban sections of our society.

It is most unfortunate to point out that Healthy Life Style especially with reference to sex education is only equated with human anatomy. It is just a narrow perception of the concept of Healthy Life Style especially relating to sex education. Inculcating self discipline and self control form the basis of Healthy Life Style. Thus implying a restructuring of educational planning to shift the emphasis from teaching to learning, because self control and self discipline are attitudes, which encourage desirable behavioural patterns to be developed in a healthy and congenial environment created by teachers, and the educational institutions, parents and the community. In other words, education should be synonymous with developing desirable attitudes and skills for adjusting well in the rapidly changing society. This, in other words, may foster the development of Healthy Life Style in students which may be conducive in the prevention of AIDS. We cannot stop the growth, the change, the revolution in the value system but we can help the youngsters to adapt to the changing system with an analytical and scientific approach. We can guide them to wisely comprehend the outcomes of accepting and discarding any set of values and ideals.

To summarize, the concept of Healthy Life Style includes development of respectful and healthy attitude towards "Sex Education" which is one of the major causes of spreading AIDS among our youngsters.

Thus, the major emphasis in this book is on introduction of sex education in schools by fostering healthy life style in students.

Sex Education : Why the Need is Urgent Now?

For centuries a frank approach to the subject of sex education has been avoided, neglected or delayed because everybody concerned with imparting such knowledge felt too embarrassed to discuss the 'secrets' of growing up, falling in love, making love – having babies, etc., etc.

And for generations things went on some how normally as sex was considered just a natural phenomenon – facts learnt instinctively. But in modern technology based society, human life cannot be just guided by instincts. The economic stress, western influence, globalization, modernization, competitive employment situation and above all a free interaction with the opposite sex necessitates the need for fostering healthy life style among our future generation especially in schools. To achieve this objective, it is imperative to impart meaningful and positive healthy sex education in our school system.

The ramifications of the modern globalization, western influence and free interaction with opposite sex are numerous. Inculcation of socially responsible behaviour, clarification of values, awareness of one's rights and responsibilities along with a tremendous amount of self discipline are mandatory for the survival of individuals and societies.

Apart from these emotional readjustments in the modern world, the emergence of HIV/AIDS in the last two decades has created almost a panic among concerned people because it is directly related to sex with an HIV virus infected person.

According to WHO and UNAIDS at the end of 2003 there were 37 million adults and 2.5 million children living with HIV. These numbers are 50% higher than the figure projected by WHO in 1991.

HIV/AIDS is a global endemic. It can infect people of any age, race, sex indiscriminately but a majority of people in the third world countries especially economically poor countries have inadequate awareness about HIV/AIDS or the ways to prevent it. The only way to control this killer virus/disease is PREVENTION through awareness because even after two decades we have not found a sure cure or a vaccine to prevent it. Just in India itself, according to the UN estimates there were 2.7 million deaths because of AIDS between 1986 and 2000. India is only second to Africa in terms of the overall number of people living with the disease. National AIDS Control Organization estimated that there were 610,000 new HIV infections in 2002.

Since young people are especially vulnerable to HIV and other sexually transmitted diseases therefore as parents and teachers it becomes obligatory to educate and prepare the young adolescents who would become sexually active and thereby face the optimum risk if they remain unaware and ignorant about the perils of Unsafe Sex. Sex Education in schools especially in the third world countries seems to be the only way to prevent the menace of HIV/AIDS, as these young people would spread the word in family, communities and villages thereby educating the illiterate adults and out of school community on the whole. Considering the fact that 60% of all new HIV infections are among 14-24 years old, can we delay the programme of sex education any further?

Fostering a Healthy Life Style is the aim of imparting sex education to the adolescents in our schools – our survival depends on their appropriate response.

What is Sex Education?

Marjorie F. Isaman defines sex education as follows:

On its simplest level, the term sex education means instructions in the basic biology of the male and female reproductive system taught in schools as a rule by classroom teacher. This term has been replaced by sexuality which means "the state or quality of sexual interest in or concern with sex".

Furthermore, the intent of school sex education is inclusion of the family; to give correct biological information, to reduce fear of sex, to put sex in a positive light and to try to upgrade moral standards.

SIECUS (Sex Information and Educational Council of the United States) defines Sex Education or Sexuality in the following manner:

> *"Connotes the totality of being, the expressing of maleness and femaleness". This term "Sex Education " has been now termed "Life Skills Education".*

Another question arises about the pedagogical aspect of sex education or Life Skills Education.

- What should be taught?
- How and when should it be taught?
- Who should teach?

To respond to the above queries (which will be discussed in the following chapters), one thing is certain that a competent and sensitive teacher is needed who can establish rapport with students. This teacher may be able to impart meaningful sex education to adolescents with reference to the above mentioned queries.

Importance of Sex Education

The importance of sex education as a means to developing a healthy personality and attitude can be proved on various counts. Sexual curiosity begins at an early age in the form of interest in physical differences between boys and girls, between adults and children. Where there is no mystery, the curiosity dies down. Sex should never be made a subject of excessive curiosity or mystery.

Sigmund Freud did a valuable service in pointing out that nervous disorders produced in later life could be due to improper teaching of young children in matters connected with sex. The suppression of sex is one of the most important causes for mental disorders in later life. Keeping things hushed up, observing secrecy and silence about the facts of sex cause them to know that their parents are telling them lies. But the adolescents gradually find out the truth sooner than their parents suppose or suspect. In an attempt to find such truths about sex, the adolescents are likely to knock at the wrong doors and thereby gather wrong information which may prove quite harmful in their later lives. Thus, adolescent sex should not be treated as a nasty, useless and tabooed subject. Ignorance, as such could lead to the unhealthy consequences or retardation in their mental development. We must ensure that our adolescents grow up healthy by learning the truth. Their emotional attitude to sex should be on the basis of clear-headed and warm - hearted contemplation of all the issues involved. A feeling of personal inadequacy underlines many sexual maladjustments. If such sexual maladjustments are reduced in number and intensity, a healthier attitude towards sex will develop. Thus, sex education may be included in the school curriculum at the secondary and senior secondary levels. To avoid controversy about "sex education", one may term it as "life skills education" or "education for life".

Action Oriented Strategies for Introducing Sex Education

The need to introduce sex education in school curricula cannot be over emphasized, considering the exposure to risks and dangers for our adolescents in the absence of proper guidance. The Educational Planners, Policy Makers and Curriculum Consultants/Developers should without any further delay get together and chalk out programmes for introducing 'Education for Life' (sex education) as a school subject at the secondary level. This should include:

A. Teacher Orientation Programme

(i) What to teach about sex-behaviour development, values, duties and responsibilities.

(ii) How to impart knowledge about sensitive issues (sex) with reference to our societal and cultural heritage.

Sex education may be included as a component of teacher education curriculum at the pre-service teacher education programme.

B. Sex Education—Education for Life

It should not just be an optional subject or a co-curricular activity. Group discussions and seminars on sex education should be arranged for teachers of all subjects and not only for the biology teachers. Students should be tested and expected to pass it as any other subject at the secondary level. Sex education content may be integrated with existing secondary school curriculum to avoid the problem of curriculum load.

The scope and sequence of curriculum of such a vast subject will have to be very flexible considering the needs, values and the socio-economic background of the students.

C. Collaboration between Mass Media and Education

A meaningful collaboration, cooperation and coordination between mass media and education sector may be made. Posters, radio, television, newspapers, cinema would have to get involved in imparting essential knowledge in appropriate manner in consultation with educationists because the media is generally responsible for exposing the adolescent to a world of fantasy through suggestions and cues.

D. Role Models for Teachers and Parents

Imparting information about sex is the very foundation of the theoretical sex education. This is best done by answering questions and removing the curiosity of the adolescents.

We must give true answers to questions asked by adolescents on social matters without suppressing facts or beating about the bush. Sex knowledge must be regarded exactly like any other knowledge of natural science or humanities. Boys and girls must be treated alike in the matter of providing information on sex. Girls should acquire adequate knowledge about sex, especially menstruation and hygiene. Boys need to learn to control their sexual urge. Both boys and girls must cultivate respect and sincerity in their relations with the opposite sex. They must learn to channel youthful energy through involvement in sports, yoga and various intellectual and creative activities.

Factual information about human anatomy and physiology is indispensable. Teaching of Biology will make clear to our adolescents that the human sex organs are essentially similar to those of other mammals. Also the difference between sexual behaviour in human and animals must be taught. Adolescents must know about venereal diseases and HIV infection/AIDS. They should be properly taught about these risks truthfully.

There is a great deal of misunderstanding in boys about masturbation, composition of semen (the main reproductive fluid) etc. The sex education course should provide not only knowledge about human anatomy, but also about 'love' as a universal human value which must include respect for the other sex, compassion, sincerity and loyalty for each other. Parents, teachers and community workers should be partners in helping the adolescents to acquire knowledge about sex.

Thus, the role of parents, teachers, doctors and community workers is quite significant. Professor Sachdeva's study (University of Newfoundland – Canada) in Indian schools points out that 47 per cent students learnt about sex from their peer group and pornographic literature; only five per cent students learn about sex from their parents. Furthermore, it is worth mentioning that teachers, if not adequately trained, will not be able to deal with the sensitive subject of sex education aptly. For meaningful sex education, it is imperative to have effective participation of teachers and parents. The main objective of imparting sex education in schools, especially among adolescents, should be to raise the level of conscience among modern male youth to encourage responsible behaviour towards their female counterparts. In reality, teachers and parents need a new orientation towards sex education, which develops a healthy approach to sex-related problems and helps the adolescents to cultivate a sense of responsibility towards the society of which they are an integral part.

The status of sex education in the West is not very encouraging due to different concept of Western morality. Virginity in the western hemisphere is not of a premium value. Western society, in general, does not frown upon illegitimate and extra marital affairs. But even the western thinking is undergoing a change. Recently, because of greater awareness about AIDS and other STDs, there has been an effort amongst certain sections of society to re-establish the institution of marriage and encourage the younger generation to commit for faithfulness towards their parents. The pre-requisite for such a concept is abstinence from sex relations before marriage.

E. Abstinence

In America, about half-million teenagers have recently signed a "True Love Waits" campaign devised by the Southern Baptist Congregation. "Believing that true love waits; I make a commitment to God, to myself, my family, my friends, my future mate and my future children to be sexually abstinent from this day, until I enter a Biblical marriage relationship."

Sex Respect and Teen Aid courses promote abstinence as the only way to prevent teen age pregnancies. It gives the impression that sex before marriage will inevitably result in disease, self-disgust, and even death. Controversial bill-boards, sponsored fundamentalists in America read: Abstinence or Death, your choice. Teen Aid also teaches basic biology and explains AIDS and HIV virus in detail. Some academicians believe that an abstinence promotion course is based upon experiment done by Gardy Memorial Hospital in Atlanta, U.S.A. The concept of abstinence is in consonance with sexual behaviour patterns and traditions in India. Manu, an Indian ancient spiritual philosopher and guide, had propagated the concept of dividing life into four stage, *viz.*, *Brahmacharya Ashram* (Adolescent stage – abstinence), *Grihasth Ashram* (Married life), *Vanaprastha*

Ashram (Ascetic life, the study of spiritual science) and *Sanyas Ashram* (the period of renunciation). The concept of abstinence is undergoing a drastic change with reference to modern values system especially in India.

F. Values Clarification and Sex Education

The essence of all knowledge is understanding the difference between right and wrong. True knowledge can be gained only by judging the values you hold and weighing them in the balance of wisdom. Values clarification, therefore, becomes the aim of education. The subject of sex education would, in fact, involve clarification of doubts, conflicts and complexes in the adolescent. The young have to be made aware of their responsibilities first of all towards themselves, secondly towards the persons they love, and thirdly towards the society in which they live and cherish their hopes and aspirations. The order of priorities would change at different times but one thing is certain that there can be no freedom without responsibility – no love without respect and no happiness without sacrifice and self control.

Our own adolescents must understand the wisdom of their forefathers and we must understand and trust our adolescents; trust that can be generated only after we have equipped them with proper knowledge to hold the torch and pass it on to the next generation.

Introduction of sex education should not be delayed any further because sex, violence and immorality have become vital influences in the young and tender minds. Consequences of indiscriminate exposure to cinema and T.V. programmes are quite apparent. Many school going adolescents find it extremely stressful to cope with the burden of the heavy curriculum load. Lack of proper guidance and self-control quite often pushes them to take drugs, get into unhealthy sexual relations or just drop out of school. These frustrated adolescents are at a great risk of falling prey to HIV/AIDS virus because they are extremely careless, inexperienced and ignorant about the pitfalls. If immediate steps are not taken to educate all adolescents (in schools and out of school) about matters concerning sex and health, we would perhaps have very little time to repent – it could be just too late for us to control the menace of AIDS and drug addiction.

To conclude, the author agrees with Freud who had aptly stumped his critics blaming him for preaching immorality through his theories of sex and dreams, stating that "when God was not ashamed of creating, why should I be ashamed of talking".

2

Sex Education in Schools

An International Perspective

What Asia can learn from Europe and Western Hemisphere?

Asia of 1990's is remarkably different from the world of 1940's especially with reference to sex related matters. There has been a tremendous openness and frankness regarding sexual permissiveness and social problems relating to sex such as sexual exploitation, sexually transmitted diseases, homosexuality, human fertility and divorce, etc. To overcome sex-related issues, problems and danger of killer disease AIDS, people in Asia have now been considering inclusion of sex instruction in the school curriculum. Let us have an overview of sex education in schools around the world from historical point of view.

Swedish Education Experience – A Unique Achievement[1-4]

Sweden was the pioneer in introducing sex education in its schools. In 1903, Dr. Karstine Widestrom was the first woman doctor who advocated compulsory sex education in Swedish schools.

Firstly, public opinion was not favourable to this kind of instruction and secondary school teachers were not adequately oriented for imparting sex instructions in schools.

However, as early as in 1936, information about sex was made compulsory in the teaching of biology in all secondary schools. The Swedish Association of Biology Teachers, founded in 1933, from its very inception was advocating sex education instructions in the schools.

Government Population Commission in Sweden recommended that sex education be introduced in few urban schools (1940).

In the mid-1950's, the above recommendation regarding introduction of sex education in schools was to be taken as a mandatory school programme. Thus, sex education was made compulsory in Sweden schools. Handbook on sex instructions in the schools was prescribed for all school teachers.

In the decades that followed the matter was raised by several Parliamentary Commissions but nothing came out of their deliberations.

Sex education in secondary schools was mainly concerned with the biology teaching till 1969, but after that a new compulsory school sex education subject was introduced in schools.

The curriculum and the Manual in Sex Education laid emphasis on sex education from biological, social, psychological and ethical point of view.

Broadly speaking, an open-minded approach to biological aspects of the sex education subject together with a comprehensive and frank consideration and respect from social and ethical point of view with different values was advocated in imparting sex education in schools.

The following were general guidelines regarding the introduction of this subject :

1. Sex instruction should be in consonance with the needs and the motivation of the people.

2. The content in sex education curriculum may include biological, sociological, psychological and ethical matter, with special reference to the accepted values of the society.

   Thus, sex education must take into consideration different wholesome views.
3. Sex education must be an integral part of teaching-learning process.

   It is only with the understanding and cooperation of parents (at local level) that schools can hope to develop meaningful sex education.

Parents and schools must work closely in this task. Parents can exert more profound moral influence on adolescents than the schools. Yet from the content point of view, especially in areas of biology, psychology, social, ethics and other related disciplines, teachers play an important role in schools. A partnership between parents and schools is the most plausible solution to the conflict anticipated by groups who are opposed to public sex education programme in schools.

Sex education programme in Swedish schools seems to have a remarkable impact on adolescents. For example, a comparative survey of the sexual knowledge of U.S., Australian, British and Swedish school children in the age group five to fifteen revealed that the Swedish children had better understanding and knowledge about sex at earlier ages than children in the other three countries.

Basis of Sex Education in Sweden

Sex education in Sweden is based on the following:

(i) *Knowledge*

The provision of correct and adequate knowledge and information about sex has been shown to be the most effective way of preventing negative effects of sexuality.

(ii) ***Frankness, Openness and Truthfulness***

Frankness, openness and truthfulness about sexual matters are most essential for adolescents to handle their own sex related issues. It provides congenial and open atmosphere for young people to clarify their questions about sex-related issues.

(ii) ***Respect for Youth***

It should be realized that young people should be given opportunities to make decisions about their own lives especially pertaining to sexual matters.

Sex education includes much more than reproduction and venereal diseases. Sex education should also give biological and psychological facts that will enrich the art of love making in couples.

It was observed that in North Korea, there was no place of sex education in the school curriculum. Even in Biology classes, there was no mention of human sex in reproduction concepts. The teachers were required to explain the concept of reproduction with reference to plants, growth of trees, rice, cotton, corn, cabbage and potatoes. The ideological situation in Communist China has been almost on the same wavelength, as in North Korea, in the area of sex education in school curriculum.

A survey of the Soviet curriculum in the late 1950's indicates that the concept of human reproductive processes was not given enough time (very little time was prescribed to the subject). Human biology was only touched. In general, there was a general aversion in the USSR regarding sex education.

Sex Education in The United States

The United States has treated inclusion of sex education in schools with a lukewarm approach, especially in mid-1930's. It was only in 1950's in Evanston, Illinois, that a pioneering programme on sex education was introduced in schools. The girls and boys were given separate instructions regarding menstruation, masturbation, homosexuality and sex organ development. Sex education programmes were introduced in New York, Anaheim, California, Jefferson County, Colorado and many other places. But in 1969, right wing groups, the Sex Information and Education Council of the United States (SIECU), opposed introduction of sex education in schools, as this may create neurons and promiscuity. Such education was not in consonance with the tenets of religion.

Sex Education in the United Kingdom (U.K.)

It is difficult to generalize introduction of sex education in the U.K. Schools as each Education Authority is autonomous; and not under the Central Government as far as curriculum development is concerned. Sex Education is considered under the 'family education programme'. The curriculum material regarding family education is developed in Nuffeld Science Programme, and Biology courses include concepts like the physiology of reproduction (human and animal). Sex education is a component of the total Nuffeld programme.

The 1944 Education Act recommended inclusion of sex education in schools. In 1944, the Board of Education (Ministry of Education) produced a pamphlet titled 'Sex Education in Schools and Youth Organization'. Since 1956, several Government reports have been produced suggesting the need for sex education, moral education and education for personal relationships. The British Broadcasting Corporation (BBC) produced several audio-visual programmes concerning sex education. The following programmes were devoted to Sex Education:

(i) Looking Ahead; a radio series devoted to Sex Education, Health and Science,
(ii) Radio programme on Health Education, Reproduction and Growth; a series of broadcasts,
(iii) 'The Science of Man'; programmes related to reproduction and birth.

Sex Education in Asia

To majority of the people in Asian sub-continent, sex is a taboo. Parents feel that imparting of sex education in schools may encourage sexual experimentation by young students. This attitude may be due to cultural heritage, societal norms and historical perspective.

Sex Education in Adolescents: Present Scenario

Adolescents today all over the world are a confused lot. They are in the process of breaking away from all that is binding, be it the family, the society or the tradition. Pride in cultural heritage has lost its significance in the shrinking global parameters. Exposure through multi-media communication system has widened the general gap overnight. Adolescents have instantly lapped up with delight whatever has appealed to them and the adults are too "helpless" and too "slow" to point out the value of rationalism and the dangers of indiscriminately borrowing ideas.

The impact of such rapid changes is being felt in every social system both progressive and conventional orthodox. Especially for a society that has stuck to its past for centuries, such sudden changes can shatter its very fabric. This is what has actually happened to the modern adolescent in India. Whereas in the West the social outlook has evolved gradually, in the third world countries, like India, there has been a superficial cultural change, merely grafting of concepts regarding sex, dating, love-making and freedom of expression. In the third world countries, the youth today is in the midst of an overwhelming 'values crisis'. The age-old customs have lost their relevance and adoption of western values is not only impractical but culturally suicidal. What the modern adolescent needs is an analytical and rational approach towards life. Only the enlightened older generation of people (parents, teachers and social workers) can guide and steer the adolescents into a world that is full of hope and not of dismay.

In India, with liberalization of economy and impact of multimedia (especially Cable T.V.), the values pertaining to permissiveness in the domain of sex related aspects would have to undergo concurrent changes. Dating and premarital sex is also on the increase. The above scenario has ramifications for sex education and sexually transmitted diseases among adolescents/youth especially at the secondary and post secondary levels.

We are all aware that AIDS is generally a sexually transmitted disease which is spreading like wild fire in Asia. The situation regarding the status of AIDS in India is very depressing. There were between 3.8 and 4.5 million Indians living with HIV/AIDS during 2002, 38.5 per cent of these were women. UN population Division projects 12.3 million AIDS deaths in India between 2000-2015.

The above alarming statistics regarding AIDS/HIV infection suggest that morally, ethically and operationally

AIDS is a global and an unprecedented challenge before all of us. It is also evident that Sex Education, especially at the school level (secondary/senior secondary level), will not be easy because of social, cultural and historical perspectives about the concept of sex education in schools but the consequences of further postponement of introducing sex education at the senior secondary school level are also very obvious.

Sex and Tradition

Science and technology have greatly changed our thinking. Sex, in the present context, is an emotional upheaval that comes into play when a boy meets a girl or vice versa. The reality of the situation today is that having sex for pleasure or production of children has become a fantasy for majority of people in India. They live in make-shift houses, crammed in urban pockets. Privacy is absolutely impossible to find. Married couples, making love during night, get shocked when they find their wards imitating them or asking queer questions. The psyche of such adolescents get mixed with so many real things that they witness, such as, movies seen on television, suggestive songs heard on the radio, or cassettes, or young people making love in isolated places, or beasts enjoying pleasure of mating on the road.

Whether our teachers teach sex at school or not, our teenagers enjoy sex by induction. Every teenage boy finds his girl friend, or vice versa, to keep their game of love alive. They fly into fantasies and into an imaginary world.

Conclusion

To conclude, one may ask the following questions:

What Asia can learn from experiences of Europe and Western Hemisphere in the area of introduction of sex education programme in schools ?

The following are some of the author's convictions which have been culled out from the learning experiences regarding sex education in the European and Western Hemisphere.

(i) Sex education in schools should not be the responsibility of biology teachers only. Sex education may include biological, sociological, psychological and ethical points of view. Thus, sex education falls in the domain of every school teacher, especially at the secondary level.

(ii) Importance of parents' cooperation in the introduction of sex education in schools cannot be over-emphasized. It is with the understanding of parents and local community that the programme of sex education can be successful as this may avoid objections.

(iii) Sex education may be based on three ingredients, *viz.*, (a) Correct knowledge about sex related matters; (b) Frankness, openness and truthfulness for transaction of sex education curriculum; (c) Respect for youth which include providing opportunities and guidance to adolescents to make their own decisions on sex related matters.

(iv) Orientation programmes for teachers may be organized in the context of transaction of sex education instructional materials. It is realized that sometimes teachers, especially female teachers, are hesitant to discuss various aspects of sex related matters such as masturbation and night-fall. These orientation programmes may include the following:

- What to teach about sex behaviour development, values, duties and responsibilities;
- How to impart knowledge about sensitive sex related issues with reference to societal and cultural heritage;
- Sexuality must be discussed in human context and not regarded as a detached and isolated part of life.
  - Sexuality education should promote sexual health, sexual rights and responsibilities.
  - Sexuality *per se* has a deep and significant human value during the entire life cycle; regardless of our age, gender or sexual disposition; and irrespective of whether we are rich or poor, healthy or handicapped; notwithstanding our nationality - whether we come from Sweden, Tanzania or Japan and so on.

Thus, sex education may be included as a component of teacher education curriculum at the pre-service and in-service teacher education programme. Furthermore, specialists in sex education may be invited to discuss sensitive sex related issues to avoid blushing and embarrassment among teachers who are supposed to transact sex related matters in school curriculum.

A meaningful collaboration, cooperation and coordination between Mass Media and Education sector may be made. For imparting essential and accurate knowledge about sex in appropriate manner, forums of radio, television and newspapers may be used appropriately.

The concept of Abstinence is worth mentioning here. In America, about half-million teachers signed a "True Love Waits" campaign devised by the Southern Baptist Congregation. Sex Respect and Teen Aid Courses promote abstinence. This concept is in consonance with sexual behaviour pattern and traditions in some of the Asian countries. For example, in India, sage Manu propagated the concept of abstinence (*Brahmacharya*). However, this concept is undergoing a drastic change with reference to modern value system.

In brief, it may be stated that Asia can learn and benefit from the experiences of other countries that have tackled successfully the programme of sex education in schools.

According to Peter Piot of UNAID "In order to prevent the spread of HIV, a combination approach is required. We need to promote abstinence, delay of sex, faithfulness and the use of condoms. No single approach will work." And for any program to be effective – information education and support are essential. This can be achieved only by taking whole heartedly the responsibility of imparting sex education in schools.

References

1. Sexology, Sexual Policy and Sex Education in Sweden (1920-30) 20th Anniversary Lecture Meeting, 1990. The Japanese Association for Sex Education, Tokyo.
2. Katraine Lindahl, *Sexuality Education from a Swedish Perspective* (RESU), August, 1995.
3. Boethus, C.G., Swedish Experiences – An Historical Perspective in *The Other Curriculum – European Strategies for School Sex Education*, editor Merdith, Philip, International Planned Parenthood Federation, 1989.
4. Steward E. Frazer (Ed), Sex, *School and Society, International Perspective,* London; Aurora Publishers, Inc. 1972.

3

Cultural Heritage and Sexual Behaviour

As we are all aware that introduction of sex education in schools is a Herculean task in the third world due to cultural, historical and religious factors, it is imperative to have an insight into the sexual behaviour patterns and traditions prevailing in a country. To substantiate the above conviction, a case in Indian sexual behaviour patterns and traditions is exemplified in the following manner:

According to the *Upanishads*, the philosophical version of the earlier *Vedas* (Hindu scriptures), sage Manu had divided life into four stages or orders:

1. ***Brahmacharya Ashram*** or the period of student life.
2. ***Grihastha Ashram*** or married life.
3. ***Vanaprastha Ashram*** or the period of ascetic life devoted to perfection of character, the study of spiritual science and divine contemplation.
4. ***Sanyasa Ashram*** or the period of renunciation devoted to the preaching of truth and righteousness to people at large and abandoning wordly connections.

The first stage *i.e., Brahmacharya Ashram* encompasses the adolescent stage. The characteristics of the *Brahmacharaya Ashram* are as follows:

- Always speak the truth;
- Lead a virtuous life;
- Abstain from sexual indulgence;
- Never be negligent in learning and teaching;

- Devote yourself to science (physical and spiritual) till your knowledge is perfect ".

To summarise, a Brahmachari (student) should abstain from sexual excitement particularly in relation to opposite sex.

- Looking upon them with an eye of lust;
- Embracing them;
- Having sexual intercourse with them;
- Reading of and talking about libidinous subjects; and
- Indulging in lascivious thoughts *i.e.*, mental intercourse with persons of opposite sex.

Thus, abstinence from sex was considered a virtue in the ancient scriptures of Indian heritage. One may " realize the self" by practicing asceticism (*tapas*) which includes abstinence from sex as an essential element.

Abstinence from Sexual Indulgence

Through the observance of '*Brahmacharya*' (total abstinence from sex in thought, word and deed), semen is converted into *ojas* and moves upward to the brain. In that case, it becomes a source of physical and spiritual strength.

Mahatma Gandhi and Sexual Abstinence

Mahatma Gandhi was a strong advocate of total sexual abstinence except for furthering generation. The following statement of Mahatma Gandhi reiterates the traditional notion about loss of energy through loss of semen (Gandhi, 1943:71):

Once the idea that the only and grand function of the sexual organ is generation, possesses men and women, union for any other purpose they will hold as criminal waste of precious energy. It is now easy to understand why the scientists of old have put such great value upon the vital fluid and why they have insisted upon its strong transmutation into the highest form of energy for the benefit of society.

Sex Sublimating to Spirituality

The traditional aspiration of sublimating sexuality into spirituality through abstinence in Hindu culture had made a strong impact on thoughts and actions of people in ancient India. Only a fraction of contemporary Hindus may practice total abstinence from sex for spiritual gain, but the theory of sublimations is widely known (Kakkar, 1989). In simple and layman's version, the theory states that 'veerya' – which stands for both vigour and semen – is the fountain of physical as well as spiritual strength and that the loss of *veerya* through sexual act or imaginary thought is not conducive for health from physical and spiritual point of view. Some believe that *veerya* can either move downward in sexual intercourse and be emitted in its gross physical form as semen or it can move upward through spinal cord to the brain in a form known as 'ojas'.

Some Common Beliefs regarding semen

According to ancient scriptures in India, food is converted into semen by successive transformations through blood. A few common assumptions are:

- 40 drops of blood produce one drop of semen;
- Each ejaculation involves a loss of half an ounce of semen which requires consumption of 60 pounds of food; and
- Each copulation is equivalent to an energy expenditure of 24 hours of concentrated mental activity or 72 hours of hard physical labour.

Modern Culture and Sexual Abstinence

The modern trend in India is to criticize the idea of preaching sexual abstinence to unmarried boys and girls in the context of prevention of AIDS and teenage pregnancy. The dominant view is that it is useless to stress sexual abstinence in sex education curricula of schools because it will simply turn off the students who are exposed to sex and violence by TV media and a large proportion of whom may have already been engaged in sexual relations. It may be advisable to see that condoms become more easily available to them by making them easily accessible. But, the author still believes that in the Indian cultural context, in the wake of special reference to rapid spread of HIV/STD infection, it may be necessary to emphasize abstinence from premarital and multiple sexual relationship in consonance with our cultural heritage as a viable option for protection from HIV infection.

Status of Pre-marital Sex among Adolescents in India

Moni Nag in his article titled "Sexual Behaviour and AIDS in India" points out about a survey conducted mainly for assessing adolescents' knowledge and attitude towards premarital sex related to family planning (FPF and ORG, 1992: 113-115). The survey was carried out in 1991 among 17,185 (13,336 male and 3,859 female) school students of 9th, 10th and 11th standards (99 per cent 18 years or under) in urban and rural areas of Uttar Pradesh, Rajasthan, Haryana and Delhi. Five per cent of male students and 3 per cent of female students were married. The frequencies of their responses to our specific statements regarding pre-marital sex are presented in Table 1.

Table 1

Responses of 17,185 Male and Female School Students to Additional Statements Regarding Premarital Sex

S. No	*Statement*	*Agree (%)*	*Disagree (%)*	*Uncertain and not specified (%)*
1.	Unmarried people should not have sexual intercourse.	51	23	26
2.	Without love, sexual intercourse is not satisfactory	35	29	36
3.	It is all right for two people to have sexual intercourse before marriage, if they are in love	28	43	29
4.	I believe in getting sexual pleasure where and when I find it.	25	41	34

Source : Compiled from FPF and ORG, 1992

The following interpretation of the finding of the study by Moni Nag is quite interesting.

The majority (51 per cent) of students agree with the statement that "unmarried people should not have sexual intercourse; but in the Indian socio-cultural context, a higher percentage would be expected to hold this view. What is quite unexpected is that 25 per cent of the students agree with the statement that "I believe in getting sexual pleasure where and when I get it". The fact that 28 per cent agree with the liberal view that "it is alright for two people to have sexual intercourse before marriage if they are in love" also reflects a trend towards liberal sexual morals among the young. The trend is reflected, however, more in views expressed by male students than those by female students. For example, 31 per cent of male students, as compared to 17 per cent of female students, agreed that it was all right for two people to have sexual intercourse before marriage if they were in love. Also 28 per cent of male students agreed with statement No. 4, while only 13 per cent of female students did so.

Other Sexual Behaviour Patterns in India

Prostitution

Prostitution or the practice of indulging in promiscuous sexual relations for money or other favours is an ancient institution in India. Kautilya's *Artha Shastra* in Circa 300 BC has aptly described the norms, behaviour, prerogatives and responsibilities about female sex workers (Basham, 1959 : 184).

Devdasi

In Hindu temples, gods were treated like kings. The idols were worshipped but it was the job of the Devdasi to attend to the gods as if they were living kings. The devdasi would dance and sing before them. Initially it was meant to be only a form of worship by dedicated religious and talented women who were born and lived in that temple only. Later the priests who even had their own wives had sex with these women (Devdasi) because they believed that they had a legitimate claim on them for serving god or gods in the temple. They considered these women to be god's gift to them for their own sexual pleasure so that they could dedicate the offspring from these women to the temple. The priests would also offer these women (Devdasi) to wealthy and influential courtiers for their generous donations to the temple. Thus, the devdasis have become victims of sexual exploitation because they have been in the profession for many generations – a normal married life for devdasi is simply not possible because of superstitions, social and religious fears and the fact that they are devdasis and not normal women. Such unfair social treatment has compelled many of them to take to prostituion and become victims of HIV/AIDS. It is gratifying to mention that the tradition of devdasi has been abolished some years ago by law.

Homosexuality

Another sexual behaviour pattern which was recognized in ancient India was homosexuality. Vatsayan's *Kama Sutra'* referred to it in connection with the practice of (oral sex by eunuchs with their male patrons and by male servants with their masters). (Burtonand Arbutnnot, 1993: 62-65).

Lesbian acts are depicted in the erotic sculptures of medieval Hindu temples (Lal 1966 : plates 67 and 68).

During the Muslim rule in India, homosexuality entered Indian court life. Some Muslim rulers are reported to have maintained harems of young boys.

The word in vogue in the western hemisphere regarding homosexual is "gay". Both male homosexuals and female homosexuals (lesbians) are classified as "gays". In modern times, it usually refers to persons whose predominant erotic inclination is towards their own sex whether or not they engage themselves in homosexual behaviour.

Hijras (Eunuch)

The commonly used English translation of the Urdu word "Hijra" is EUNUCH. A less commonly used translation is intersexual (hermaphrodite). Eunuch refers to a castrated (emasculated) male and intersex refers to a person whose genitals are ambiguously male like at birth. Impotence is the force behind both the English words but is only a necessary and not sufficient condition for being recognized as hijra in India.

Hijras are popular in the northern parts of India where they carry on their traditional roles of dancing and singing in homes on occasions of male childbirth, wedding and other festivals.

Anthropologists believe that in addition to their traditional cultural role as performers for means of livelihood, Hijras also engage in sexual activity with men for money or for satisfying their own sexual desires.

Sexual Morality from Catholic Church Resources points of view has been aptly described by Dr. George Palackapilly, SDB, Secretary, in the following manner:

Male and Female He Created Them . . .

God is love, creating the human race in his own image ...., God inscribed in the humanity of man and woman the capacity and responsibility, to love and to pro-create.

The Bible tells us that "When God created man, he made him in the likeness of God. Male and female he created them, and he blessed them and named them Man when they were created".

Sexuality affects all aspects of the human person in the unity of his body and soul. It especially concerns effectively, the capacity to love and to procreate, and in a more general way the aptitude for making bonds of communication with others.

Everyone, man and woman, should acknowledge and accept his sexual identity. Physical, moral, and spiritual differences and complementarity are oriented towards the goal of marriage and the flourishing of family life. The harmony of the couple and of the society depends in part on the way in which the complementarity, needs and mutual support between the sexes are lived out.

Each of the two sexes is an image of the power and tenderness of God with equal dignity though in a different way. The union of man and woman in marriage is a way of imitating in the flesh the Creator's generosity and fecundity "Therefore a man leaves his father and his mother and cleaves to his wife, and they become one flesh." All human generations proceed from this union.

Jesus came to restore creation to the purity of its origins In the Sermon on the Mount, he interprets God's plan strictly You have heard that it was said, "You shall not commit adultery'. But I say to you that everyone who looks at a woman lustfully has already committed adultery with her in his heart."

Chastity

Chastity means the successful integration of sexuality within the person and thus the inner unit of man in his bodily and spiritual being. Sexuality, in which man's belonging to the bodily and biological world is expressed, becomes personal and truly human when it is integrated into relationship of one person with another is the complete and lifelong mutual gift of a man and a woman.

The chaste person maintains the integrity of the powers of life and love placed in him. This integrity ensures the unit of the person; it is opposed to any behaviour that would impair it. It tolerates neither a double life nor duplicity in speech.

Chastity includes an apprenticeship in self-mastery which is a training in human freedom. The alternative is clear: either man governs his passions and finds peace, or he lets himself be dominated by them and becomes unhappy. Man's dignity, therefore, requires him to act out of conscious and free choice, as moved and drawn in a personal way from within, and not by blind impulses in himself or by mere external constraint.

Self-mastery is a long and exciting work. One can never consider it acquired once and for all. It presupposes renewed effort at all stages of life. The effort required can be more intense in certain periods, such as when the personality is being formed during childhood and adolescence.

Chastity blossoms in friendship. God is our Father and Friend. It is expressed notably in friendship with one's neighbour. Whether it develops between persons of the same or opposite sex, friendship represents a great good for all.

People should cultivate chastity in the way that is suited to their state of life. Some profess virginity or celibacy which enables them to give themselves to God alone with an undivided heart in a remarkable manner. Others live in the way prescribed for all by the moral law, whether they are married or single. Married people are called to live in conjugal chastity; others practice chastity in continence.

Offences against Chastity

Lust is disordered desire for or inordinate enjoyment of sexual pleasure. Sexual pleasure is morally disordered when sought for itself, isolated from its procreate and unitive purposes.

By masturbation is to be understood the deliberate stimulation of the genital organs in order to derive sexual pleasure. Down the centuries, the Catholic Church has firmly maintained that masturbation is an intrinsically and gravely disordered action.

Fornication is carnal union between an unmarried man and an unmarried woman. It is gravely contrary in the dignity of persons and of human sexuality which is naturally ordered to the good of spouses and the generation and education of children.

Moreover it is a grave scandal when there is corruption of the young.

Pornography consists in removing real or stimulated sexual acts from the intimacy of the patterns, in order to display them deliberately to third parties. It offends against chastity because it perverts the conjugal act, the intimate giving of spouses to each other. It does grave injury to the dignity of its participants (actors, vendors, public), since each one becomes an object of base pleasure and illicit profit for others. It immerses all who are involved in the illusion of a fantasy world. It is a grave offence. Civil authorities should prevent production and distribution of pornographic materials.

Prostitution does injury to the dignity of the person who is engaged in it, reducing the person to an instrument of sexual pleasure. The one who pays sins gravely against himself. Prostitution is a social scourge. It usually involves women, but also men, children and adolescents.

Rape is the forcible violation of the sexual intimacy of another person. It does injury to justice and chastity. Rape deeply wounds the respect, freedom and physical and moral integrity to which every person has a right. It causes grave damage that can mark the victim for life. It is always an intrinsically evil act. Graver still is the rape of children committed by parents (incest) or those responsible for the education of the children entrusted to them.

Chastity and Homosexuality

Homosexuality refers to relations between men or between women who experience an exclusive or predominant sexual attraction towards persons of the same sex. It has taken a great variety of forms through the centuries and in different cultures. Its psychological genesis remains largely unexplained. Basing itself on sacred scripture, which presents homosexual acts as acts of grave depravity, tradition has always declared that "homosexual acts are intrinsically disordered". They are contrary to the natural law. They close the sexual act to the gift of life. They do not proceed from a genuine attractive and sexual complementarity. Under no circumstances can they be approved.

Teenage Sex : Yes or No

The world presents the teenager with contradictory message about sex. Parents and religious leaders teach that sex should be saved for marriage and that pre-marital sex is sinful. The TV, cinema, music and press say that sex is great fun and perhaps everyone is having it.

Where does the teenager stand?

Perhaps some teenagers are already saying "yes" to pre-martial sex. Some feel pressured into having sex. Some give in to be popular, or to be with or keep someone's love, or to prove something to someone. Some are just curious and want to find out what it is like. Some use sex for comfort or reassurance. Some teenagers are drunk or high when they have sex.

Is it true that everyone is doing it? The answer is NO.

Some teens choose not to have sex because they want to avoid pregnancy, AIDS and other diseases. Some are afraid of sex, or afraid of getting caught or afraid of feeling guilty afterwards.

Religious convictions keep many teens away from sex. They see sex as a precious gift of God and want to preserve it for married life only.

Real Love

Some teens say it is all-right to have sex if you really love each other. Love is a very elusive reality. Love can easily be confused with infatuation and even exploitation. And that brings us to the question of what is real love?

Love is patient, kind, willing to excuse the faults of others; love is not jealous or boastful. Love demands commitment. Most teenagers admit that they are not ready for the kind of long term commitment that is required in marriage.

Sex without real love will not make one happy. Without love, sex is a source of problems, worry, guilt, heartache, pain and disappointment. If one really loves other person, he should be prepared to say No to sex until their love is committed in to marriage.

A full sexual commitment is such an important decision that both civil law and church law have a special process to publicize and formalize the commitment. That is what the marriage vow is a formal commitment to accept all the responsibilities that accompany a sexual union.

Teenagers sometime ask: Is it not possible for sexual intercourse to help to keep a relationship growing?

Though most of the songs and movies and love stories present a cosy picture of such relationships, experience tells us that it is not so. Too early sex seldom helps a relationship to grow. Premature sex is much more likely to destroy a relationship than deepen it. Intense infatuation leading to sex is not real love. It can easily end up in exploitation of one partner by the other.

Sometimes teenagers think that "everybody is doing it", especially the more popular teenagers. The fact is that the majority of teenagers are not in relationships involving sexual intercourse. Young people who are well adjusted, highly motivated and future oriented are far less likely to be sexually active than those with a low self concept and low ideals.

Safe Sex

Many teens and adults in order to avoid the risks of extra material sex like unwanted pregnancy, STD, AIDS etc., advocate "safe sex", that is, use contraceptives.

The moral teachings of the church and the norms of modern society do not agree in the area of contraception. The social community generally accepts the use of contraceptives by adults. The church does not.

Modern society, however, is divided about the wisdom of giving contraceptives to teenagers. Some adults feel that the way to protect teens from pregnancy and sexually transmitted diseases is to make contraceptives easily available to them, even dispensing them in educational institutions.

Others are of the opinion that giving teenagers easy access to contraceptives increases the problems connected with teenage sexual activity. Statistics show that the number of teenage pregnancies and abortions has gone up rather than coming down when contraceptive devices are made easily available to the teenagers.

The Catholic Church teaches that sexual intercourse is to be practised only within marriage. Therefore, the only form of contraception that is moral outside marriage is abstinence.

How safe are Contraceptives?

Contraception is not a safe way for teens to avoid risks. It is also risky in itself.

The very act of buying contraceptive acts is against the personal moral standards of most teens. Most teens feel guilty about the secrecy and duplicity required to hide contraceptives from their parents.

The rate of effectiveness of contraceptives decreases when the user is young, inexperienced and not under a doctor's supervision. The use of non-use of contraceptives can be a constant source of contention, suspicion and conflict in relationship.

> *Many sexually-active teens do not have enough knowledge or maturity to assume the regular responsibility required to make contraception even minimally effective. Safe sex is not safe. There are no short cuts. The only cent per cent protection against the dangers connected with sex is continence, that is, to reserve sexual activity for marriage.*

Purification of the Heart

> *The heart is the seat of moral personality : "Out of the heart comes evil thoughts, murder, adultery, fornication........". The struggle against carnal covetousness entails purifying the heart and practicing temperances..*

In the Sermon on the Mount Jesus proclaimed, "Blessed are the pure in heart, for they shall see God". "Pure in heart" refers to those who have attuned their intellects and wills to the demands of God's holiness. Purity of heart is the precondition to see God face to face. It lets us perceive the human body-ours and our neighbour's – as a manifestation of divine beauty.

Purity requires modesty, an integral part of temperance. Modesty protects the intimate centre of the person. It means refusing to unveil what should remain hidden. It is ordered to Chastity to whose sensitivity it bears witness. It guides how one looks at others and behaves towards them in conformity with the dignity of persons and their solidarity.

Modesty is decency. It inspires ones choice of clothing. It keeps silence or reserved where there is evident risk of unhealthy curiosity. It is discreet.

There is a modesty of the feelings as well as of the body. It protects, for example, against the voyeuristic explorations of the human body in certain advertisements, or against the solicitations or certain media that go to fare in the exhibition of intimate things. Modesty inspires a way of life which makes it possible to resist the allurements of fashion and the pressures of prevailing ideologies.

Purity requires purification of the social climate. It requires of the communications media that their presentations should show concern for respect and restraint. Purity of heart brings freedom from wide spread eroticism and avoids entertainment inclined to voyeurism and illusion.

The so-called moral permissiveness rests on an erroneous understanding of human freedom. True freedom is developed through education in the moral law. Those in-charge of education should truthfully instruct young people about the qualities of heart and mind and moral and spiritual dignity of man.

Contents and Strategies of Sex Education among Adolescent Girls and Boys

Sex education for adolescents in the school system is a very controversial issue due to our historical and cultural perspectives. The following questions arise in one's mind – what should be its contents? What may be the acceptable strategies for imparting it? Contents and strategies of sex education should be need based with reference to interest and absorbing capacity of adolescents.

In terms of prevention of AIDS/STD, it is important to give top priority to sex education in schools especially at the secondary level. Sexual terminologies, easily comprehensible to these adolescents, need special exploration. Experimental research methods may be useful to identify the contents and strategies of sex education best suited for adolescents at the secondary school stage.

4

Adolescents and AIDS

In all rapidly changing societies, the behaviour pattern of younger generations is affected greatly by the conflicting values. In the past the younger generation in India accepted with reverence the morals and ideals of their elders and had unquestioning faith in the ancient wisdom of our elders and ancestors. Not too long ago religion alone shaped every facet of human activity in India. With the erosion of these centuries' old values not only among our adolescent but in elders also, the social structure of this nation is in turmoil. With the impact of satellite television, videotapes and mass media, the adolescents are going through a tremendous value crises. The adolescents especially from urban population had been imbibing western cultural values in the last few decades and now they are adopting these alien values with unforeseen passion. A few years ago talking about sex among adolescents was taboo. Pre-marital sex and extra-marital affairs were not accepted by the societal norms but there were instances, which became the subject of fiction and scripts for films. In fact that was what the average person liked to believe and deviation from normal accepted moral codes was thought to be a writer's fantasy.

Now with the growing disregard and rejection of traditional values, the young adolescents are setting up their own code of ethics and a new set of morals in matters of sex, love, dating and life in general. It becomes obligatory for the educators, and social scientists to study the ramifications of such behaviour patterns. The task becomes even more complicated in the case of a vast number of out-of-school adolescents.

A study conducted by a group of medical professionals and social scientists of the All India Institute of Medical Sciences in1994 is quite revealing.

The sample of the study comprised of six schools of South Delhi. A total of 716 (303 girls and 413 boys) students, generally 16-17 years old, were questioned. An overview of questions and answers is as follows:

1. Do you think students of your age have sex?

   Yes (Boys) 63%

   Yes (Girls) 37%

   Boys said students of their age have sex generally with prostitutes or known older women.
2. How often do you think students of your age have sex:

   Often 9%, Occasionally 20%, Rarely 26%

   Don't know 45%
3. Do students of your age have sex with a partner of the same sex;

   Yes 15%

   No 33%

   Don't know 52%
4. Are you prepared to risk AIDS rather than miss the chance of having sex with an attractive stranger ?

   Yes (Boys) 19%

   (Girls) 9%

   Don't know 17%
5. If you want to know something about sex, whom would you like to contact :

   Friends 44%

   Doctor 42%

   Parents 12%

   Teachers 2%

6. Kissing can result in AIDS ... 27%
7. AIDS can be cured if detected early ... 37%
8. Only prostitutes get AIDS ... 19%
9. Only homosexuals get AIDS ... 12%
10. I am not the type of persons to get AIDS .. 67%
11. Won't eat in a restaurant if someone working there has AIDS ... 38%
12. If a student in school has AIDS – others should be informed ... 60%
13. Sharing of towels or clothes can transmit sexually transmitted diseases (STD) ... 54%
14. There is no treatment for STDs ... 20%
15. AIDS can be caused by donating blood ... 41%
16. Not to visit a friend who has AIDS ... 32%

Even though the above statistics are just indicative, they have alarming ramifications because these adolescents are indulging only in casual sex. They are too young to go for permanent relations. The other danger is lack of having a safe sex since the act is done in complete secrecy and in an unplanned manner. Thirdly, as the sexual activity for them is a mere game, they could be changing partners quite frequently, thus exposure to AIDS and STD is optimum. Furthermore, with the vast migratory population of rural adolescents to big cities, this problem is quite complex. The conclusion from the above deliberation is quite obvious, *i.e.*, there is a dire need for sensitization of adolescents (school as well as out -of -school) about AIDS/HIV infection with special reference to sex and drug abuse.

For all those who are involved in educating adolescents, it is imperative to provide basic information about AIDS.

Basic Information about AIDS

The body health is defended by its immune system. White blood cells called Lymphocytes – B and T cells –

protect the body from foreign agents (such as viruses, bacteria, parasites and fungi).

When germs are detected and cells are activated. This process is hindered in case of Acquired Immuno Deficiency Syndrome (AIDS).

Thus AIDS is a disease in which the body's immuno system breaks down. AIDS is caused by Human Immuno Deficiency Virus (HIV).

When HIV enters the body it infects special T cells where the virus grows. The virus kills these cells slowly. As more and more of the T cells die, the body's ability to fight infection weakens.

Measuring the number of CD4 Lymphocytes is the primary test for monitoring immune functions:

It establishes the stage of HIV infection, the prognosis is of disease.

The number of CD4 cells should be measured once every six months when the CD4 count is greater than 600 cells/ml and at least once in every three months when CD4 unit is between 20 cells/ml and 600 cells/ml. More frequent measurement may be desirable if there is evidence of rapid decline in cell count.

The re-emergence of tuberculosis (TB) as a major public health concern is especially important for HIV infected individual because there is likelihood of development of active TB.

AIDS knows no boundaries, or discrimination. The virus attacks male/female of any ethnicity and colour – gay, lesbians or heterosexual. Incubation period may range from 2 to 10 years depending upon person's capacity to resist the virus. A person with HIV infection may remain healthy for many years. HIV was first identified in 1984 by French and American scientists but the human immuno deficiency virus did not get its name until 1986.

The World Health Organisation (WHO) had predicted that 30 to 40 million men, women, and children around the world would be infected with the human immuno deficiency virus (HIV) by the year 2000. But the actual numbers in 2003 were 50% higher than the projected figures. Therefore, the growing population of HIV infected individuals need guidance, adequate care and due attention.

HIV Infection and Illnesses

AIDS diagnoses : People suffering from full developed AIDS symptoms result in the breakdown of the immune system.

Symptoms of AIDS

(a) Unexpected weight loss
(b) Enlarged glands
(c) Night sweats
(d) Swollen lump glands in the neck, armpit or groin
(e) Diarrhea, fever, chill
(f) Dry cough
(g) In some cases, a severe temporary illness.

Transmission of HIV Infection through Sex

1. Coition – Engaging in Vaginal, and/or oral sex.
2. Oral sex particularly if there are breaks in the skin.
3. Heterosexual with safe sexual practices.
4. HIV positive women can transmit the virus to new born babies, a pre-natal symptom.

The other modes of transmission include blood transfusion and drug abuse through needles and syringes.

To sum up, any activity which includes the transfer of saliva, sputum-infected blood, semen or vaginal fluids from an infected person into the blood stream of another person can be a source of HIV infection.

Who can get it?

(a) Homosexual/Bisexual
(b) Heterosexual without safe enjoyment methods.
(c) Drug users (Especially using drugs intravenously).
(d) People getting blood transfusions – if the donor blood is infected. It often happens in developing countries that the donors are not screened for HIV infection.

A Few Pointers

(a) Avoid mixing with multiple partners.
(b) Use condom to prevent exchange of body fluid from start to finish.

Counselling for HIV positive individual may need immediate intervention with reference to mental, social and family.

Some infected individuals may not like to disclose their HIV positive status but they should be encouraged to do so as this may be significant particularly with sexual and needle bearing partner. But the disclosure needs educating parents and guidance at their places of work. This may also require periodic comprehensive physical check up which may include eye, oral health, neuralgic status, skin and lymph nodes and HIV associated signs and symptom.

Females are more AIDS Prone

The following are some factors which contribute to transmission of AIDS in females more than male.

(i) *Perverted Sexual Practice*
Females are generally subjected to perverted sexual practices and sometimes are victims of prosecution and rape.

(ii) *Poor Health Conditions*
Females generally have poor health conditions than the male counterparts.

(iii) *Higher Illiteracy Rate*
There is higher illiteracy rate among females than males.

(iv) *Neglect of Health*
Females especially with HIV positive symptoms generally neglect their health.

A recent study in Mumbai has shown 30:1 ratio for female to male for HIV infection.

Preventing AIDS through Love/Sex as a Human Value

Due emphasis has to be given on the dynamics of "love making", or "making love" is to be taken as a universal human value which should inculcate respect for other sex, compassion, sincerity and loyalty for each other *i.e.*, male/female. Mahatma Gandhi's concept of love is very appropriate in this context which suggests that when we say we love someone, we are supposed to respect that person *i.e.*, his feelings, sentiments and values. There is no love when there is no respect. Concept of love has been aptly described by late Krishnamurti, reputed international spiritual leader, in the following paragraph:

> *You do not say, "I love the whole world", but when you know how to love one, you know how to love*

> *the whole world. Because we do not know how to love one, and love of humanity is fictitious. When you love, there is neither one not many, only love.*

Meslow describes love as a part of being human *i.e.*, "The need for love characterizes every human being that is born".

Montague defines love as "one's needs are satisfied by persons whom one loves".

As mentioned earlier the modern adolescent youth in India is in the midst of value crises. The traditional values are being replaced by modern values. Thus, the confusion and conflict result in literally tearing apart the culture of the modern generation in India. Does it have to be an either/or choice. Isn't it possible for our modern youth/adolescent to amalgamate the best ideas from their own cultures and that of the West? How does one accomplish this task?

A promising approach for dealing with the emerging values crisis among the youth is the rejection of the ideas of imposing the right "values" upon them. Instead one can teach them a process and a set of criteria by which they can themselves evaluate the soundness of their values. The approach might give the youth a set of tools and skills for sorting out the alternatives which are available and the consequences which may result, if they continue to live with a focus on their values.

Thus, the "love" as a value may indicate that sex before marriage is not very desirable especially without taking precautions of safe sex. If the above concept of sex is not followed sexual mode of contracting AIDS/HIV virus may occur.

Evidently our society and its values are rapidly changing. The modern youth questions the values of his parents, teachers and leaders. If one is to cope with these changing attitudes, it is imperative to discuss the importance of values in the changing scenario. Values are acquired by examples and transmitted by what we do, not by what we say we should do. If we do not accept the concept of sex in terms of "love" as a value, especially with reference to safe sex, it may be futile to discuss or preach the same to our modern generation. If we are to develop a process of assessing values, we must understand the background and environment of the youth. We need to provide them with opportunities to test their values. Errors in judgement may be discussed. But the older generation must be prepared to accept values that the youth derive from the modern situation. The following strategies for such values clarification may be quite helpful in overcoming the "value crisis" with special reference to sex issues.

These may include : (i) Problem solving; (ii) Scientific method in values questions; (iii) My favourite activities; (iv) Discouraging apathy; (v) Comparing values; (vi) Rating values; (vii) Where do you stand?; (viii) In-between issues; (ix) On the spot decisions, I am proud; (x) In the public eyes; (xi) Sharing experiences. Learning to listen; (xii) What are the consequences?; (xiii) Slicing the apple of your life; (xiv) Make a wish, What am I ?; (xv) Picture of my life, and (xvi) Communication lines etc.

The authors have discussed in detail the above values clarifications and other sex related matters in the preceding chapters.

5

Inculcation of Human Values amongst Students

To foster healthy life style among students for prevention of AIDS, it is imperative to inculcate human values among students in the school system. In ancient societies religion was the ruling force in every sphere of human life. Education was primarily value oriented based on religious dictums. Today when secularism is expected to be the basic ideology of all progressive democratic countries, the task of providing moral education without any reference to a particular religion is a challenge for the educators. At the same time there is the need at present for inculcation of values because of diminishing influence of religion, absence of elders in the nuclear family and individualism resulting in an unprecedented erosion in the values of the younger generation.

Values — Definition

The dictionary meaning of the term value is something that has worth, utility and importance. From a historical view point, a value may be defined as a thing which is good. Operationally, the concept of values may be defined as "factors which affect human behaviour".

Intellectually, value may be defined as a "concept which is accepted by the sub-conscious mind, is understood by all and perceived by the individual."

When we talk of human values, we generally refer to factors which affect human behaviour and emotional attitude. Thus, human behaviour is guided by values. The self centred individual of today puts personal gain (in monetary terms) as a single guiding value in his life and which can be detrimental for the society. Therefore, when we are striving for inculcating human values in education, our aim is to outline and manifest those values which would bring happiness to the individual and would be beneficial for the society and mankind as well.

Catagories of Values

Values may be categorized as follows:

(1) Essential values—These involve the basic nature of man himself.
(2) Personal values—What is profitable and good for the individual.
(3) Social values—What is good for the society. It discusses the basis of the relationship of the individual with other people.
(4) Cultural values—Which involve the survival of the culture.
(5) Institutional values—Which include the political values, the moral values and establishment values.

Other questions arise :

(i) Do the values themselves change?
(ii) Is it only our interpretation of constant values that change?

One can assume, that abstract values such as tolerance, self-respect, love, truth and patriotism remain constant. However, world events may bring about changes in priorities. During the Vietnam War, in the U.S.A., Draft dodging was considered by many as a sign of patriotism in comparison to going to war.

Furthermore, our rapidly changing society results in a constant reassessment of our values. Science, once regarded

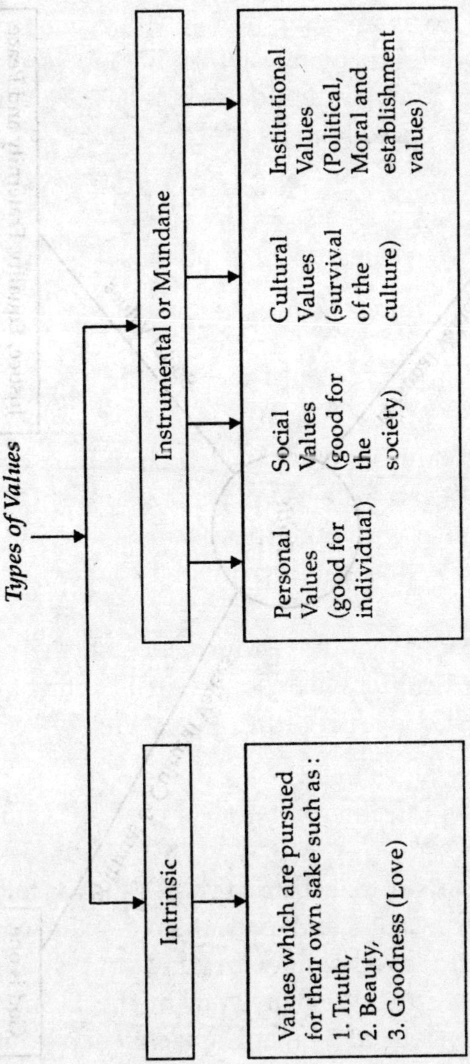

Figure 1 : Types of Values

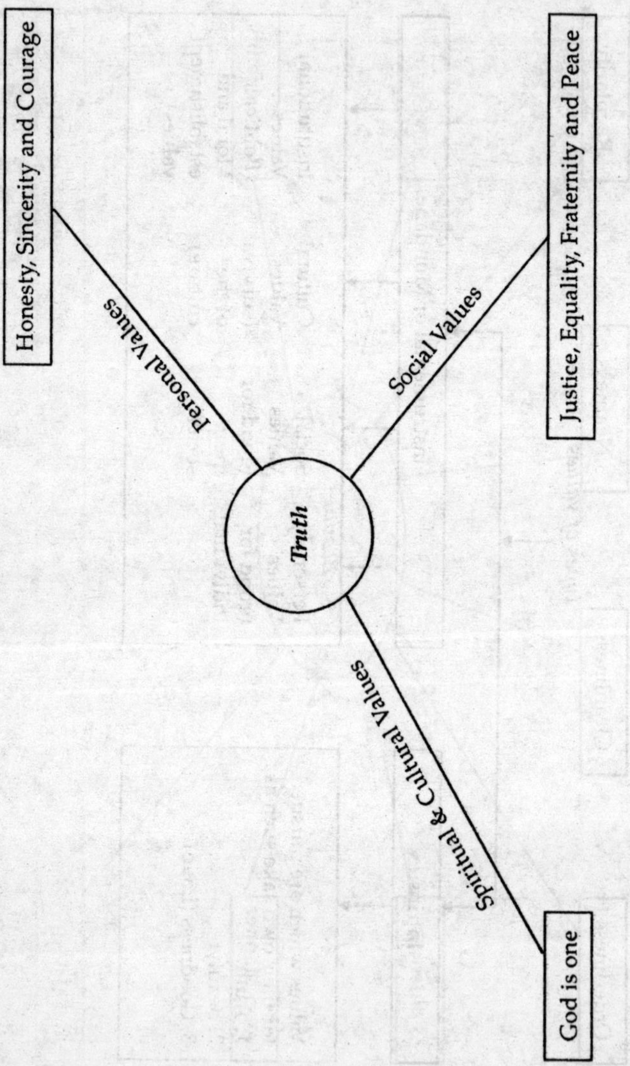

Figure 2 : Truth

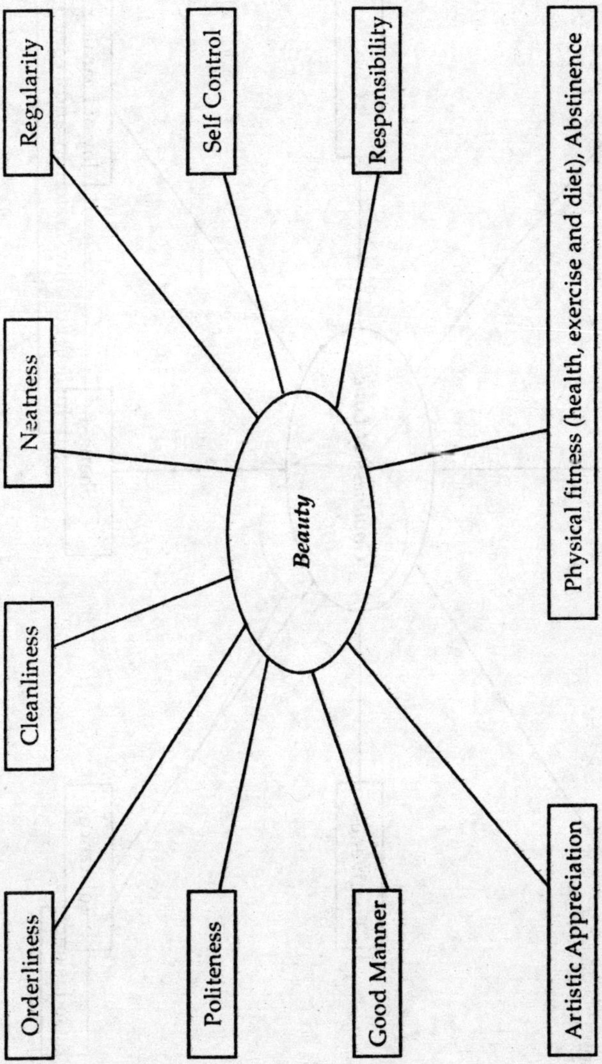

Figure 3 : Beauty

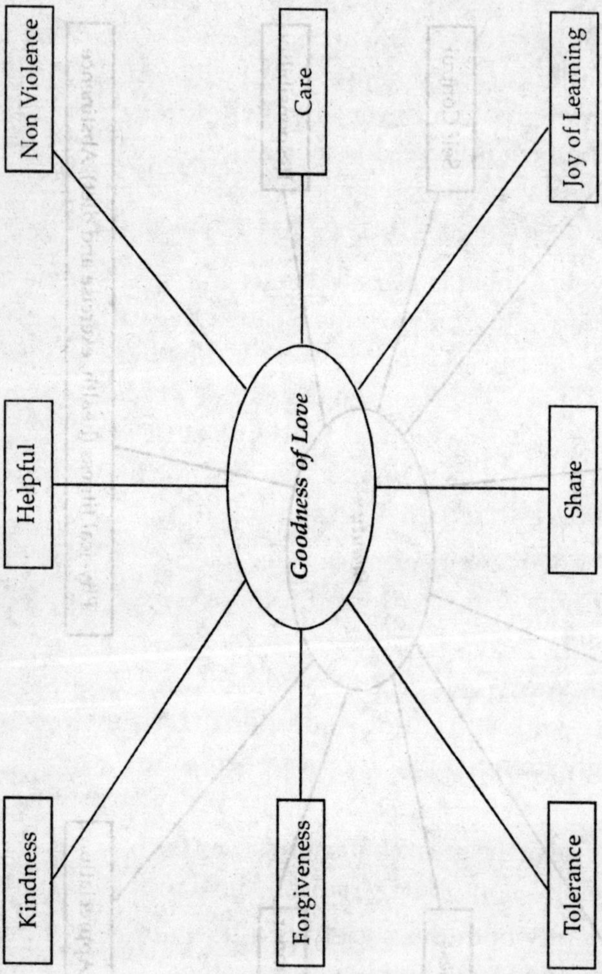

Figure 4 : Goodness of Love

All these values promote Healthy Life Style among students which may prevent Drug Abuse and AIDS among students.

as wholly beneficial, has undergone a subtle value change in recent years. With its ramifications affecting the social, educational and political issues of our time, science has acquired an un-savoury characterization. The fact that we have the technical know-how to destroy the world, whether quickly through atomic war or slowly through pollution and environmental abuse, does not improve science's image. But we have not developed human values which may control the above destruction. Thus, we feel threatened.

However, there is a great danger in regarding science as a singular value system. If the weakness of various ethnic cultures is their resistance to scientific thinking, then there has been equal stubborness on the part of western scientific culture to be over-committed to technology. The historical records of all great civilizations show that cultural idealism and technology must exist side by side.

The great engineering master pieces in all ethnic cultures testify that science and technology are thousands of years old.

What Westerners call the "industrial revolution" was in reality only an unprecedented acceleration and exceedingly strong emphasis on a particular aspect of human activity.

The rise of the great civilizations was not brought about by technology alone, but by radically new social inventions.

Evidently both our society and its values are rapidly changing. Modern youth questions the values of their parents. If we are to cope with these changing attitudes, it is imperative to discuss the importance of values in our school system.

But, there is no need to Preach and Teach values to the youngsters. Once they understand these basic values, the relevance of these will be self evident. The child has learnt to appreciate all that truthful, beautiful and good and discard things and behaviour which are undesirable.

Values in the School System

Different sets of values are to be encouraged/inculcated at different stages of school education.

Values at the Primary Level

The list of Values is as under —

1. Joy of Learning, 2. Love – Love for mother, father, friend, teacher, nature, animals, schools, home and country, 3. Care, 4. Share, 5. Co-operate, 6. Helping others, 7. Forgiveness, 8. Obedience, 9. Cleanliness, 10. Orderliness, 11. Good Manners, 12. Politeness, 13. Respect for Elders, 14. Kindness, 15. Honesty, 16. Courage, 17. Fearlessness, 18. Pride in own culture.

Strategies for Inculcation of Values at Primary Level

Following strategies should be adopted —

- Exemplary behaviour of the teacher
- Demonstrating good manners, respect for elders and discipline (School and Home)
- Prayer (Meaning of the Prayer)
- Celebration of special days and festivals relating to different religions, national and international days
- Charts and pictures in the class
- Frequent meeting with parents

Values at the Secondary Level

These are as under—

1. Knowledge, 2. Scientific Temper, 3. International understanding, 4. Spiritual Strength, 5. Patriotism, 6. Justice,

7. Sincerity, 8. Honesty, 9. Courage, 10. Respect for fair sex, 11. Patience, 12. Good conduct, Abstinence, 13. Tolerance, 14. Broadness of vision, intuition, 15. Development of grace, beauty, strength, and beauty of the soul and mind.

Character Formation and Assessment of Values

Today the youngsters are in "Values Crisis". Whether to accept "Western Values" in toto or 'rejection of traditional values' is a "crisis" issue.

Values are acquired by examples and these values are transmitted (caught) by what we do, not what we say to do. Teachers may be oriented with different strategies for assessing values.

1. *My Favourite Activities*
   Helping the student to examine his favourite activities, e.g., writing down fifteen things you like to do.
2. *Discouraging Apathy*
   To develop stronger and clearer point of view. Describing views about important issues like poverty and corruption.
3. *Comparing Values*
   To give a chance to see how others value things.
4. *Rating Values*
   Making decision of different degrees. Publicly stating his views and defending them.
5. *Where do you stand?*
   To determine strength of your feelings on certain values. Have a ladder of series of steps drawn in their notebooks.
6. *I am Proud*
   To build self confidence in the student. Your pride in relation to certain aspects of life.

Human Universal Values
(Truth, Beauty and Goodness as Root Values)

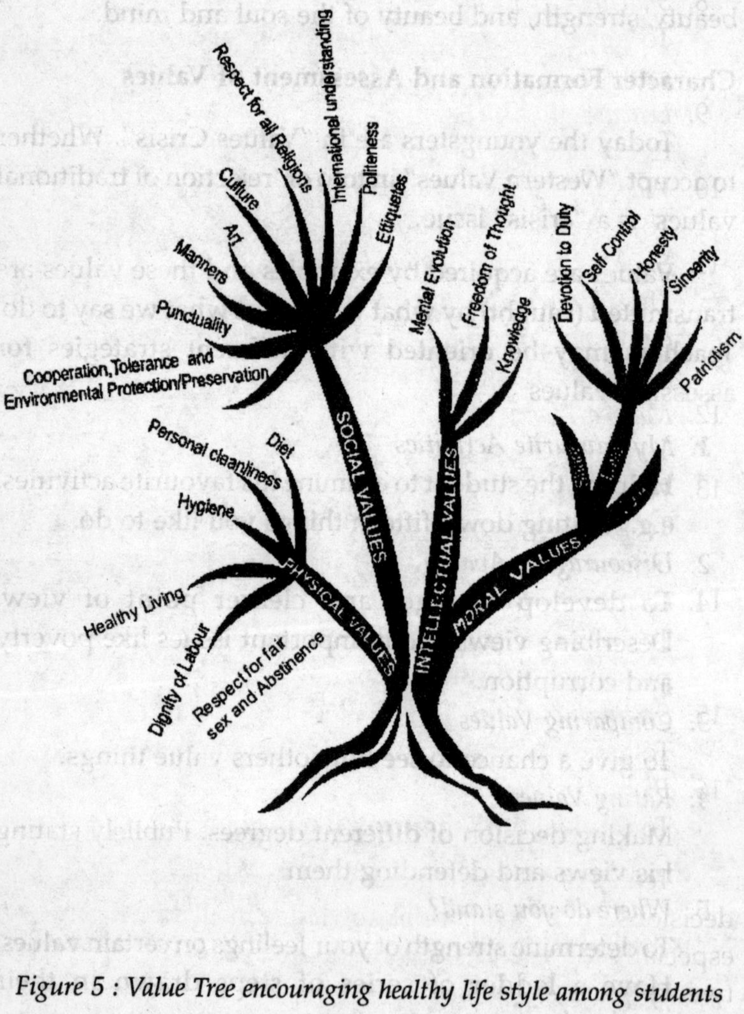

Figure 5 : Value Tree encouraging healthy life style among students

7. *In the Public Eye*
   To give a person the chance to state his views in the classroom.
8. *Sharing Experience*
   To get to know each other by interviews in a small group.
9. *Learning to Listen*
   Every one has a right to express their own values.
10. *What are the Consequences*
    To search for consequences.
11. *Slicing the Apple of your Life*
    How do you spend your time and money? Draw a circle on your paper and divide it into four quarters depicting the life style.
12. *Make a Wish*
    To make you think about your value.
13. *What Am I?*
    To know yourself better. To think about your life objectively.
14. *Chapters of My Life.*
    To see your life as a whole to think of goals-past, present and future.
15. *Strength of Beliefs*
    To assess how strongly you believe in something.
16. *Picture of My Life*
    To think about where my life is going.

Teachers face an increasing number of curriculum decisions. An avalanche of knowledge in all academic areas, especially the sciences, has thundered upon man in the last twenty years.

How can teachers supply meaningful educational experiences for children in the light of this explosion in knowledge? Can teachers change the content of teaching in order to better meet the needs of their students, their communities, and their society? That this is a difficult, if not an impossible task for teachers to accomplish, is abundantly clear.

Furthermore, recent educational innovations have overlooked human growth. Instead of using modern "jargon" (such as programmed instruction, differentiated staffing, individualized learning and behavioural objectives), our emphasis should be on child growth and development. Human growth is directly related to the "Values" development among the children.

Students in developing countries are in the midst of an overwhelming "values" crisis. Seeking more of what western technology and culture can produce, some of the students push for adoption of western ideas and practices. They are faced with a choice; either staying as they are or adopting the western value system in total and rejecting everything they have known. This confusion and conflict results in literally tearing apart the cultures of the children.

Does it have to be either Choice?

Isn't it possible for children to amalgamate the best ideas from their own culture and that of the West's?

Teachers must provide a learning environment which affords both experiences desired by the child as well as a basis for the formal education goals of the schools.

How does one accomplish this task?

A promising approach for dealing with the emerging values crisis among the students is the rejection of the idea of imposing "right" values upon them. Instead we teach them a process and a set of criteria by which they can arrive at and evaluate the soundness of their own values. This approach might give students a set of tools and skills for sorting out the alternatives which are available and the consequences which may result as they continue to live with a focus on their values.

The school, then, is one of the most appropriate places where "value" concept can be fully expanded. A teacher must demonstrate those values in which he/she believes. In order to discuss the values related question in the class, it is imperative to have a better understanding of human growth. Class rooms and schools should provide proper environment for our children to develop some of the following qualities.

(i) Trust
(ii) Honesty
(iii) Patience
(iv) Flexibility
(v) Understanding
(vi) Self respect
(vii) Real Love
(viii) Respect for others especialy fair sex
(ix) Abstinence

However the question that now arises is: Should the development of the above mentioned qualities be at the expense of the mastery of subject matter?

Some educators feel that the school can provide value lessons, only at the expense of factual knowledge. Others feel that "Value" questions should be incidental. It is quite difficult to polarize factual knowledge and human growth. It is not an either/or question, but both processes should work hand in hand. We, as educators, should not lay emphasis on one aspect at the cost of another. Our schools have a responsibility to the community to foster community values *i.e.*, to lead our children to understand and accept the values accepted by the society within which the school operates. Socially accepted value systems may be developed through self discovery. This implies the designing of a curriculum which caters to the needs of the community and overcomes the conventional gap between school knowledge and life situations. Thus, the philosophy of any school programme may be based on a new system of education that will enable high school students to develop skills, acquire knowledge which will enrich their life, and lead them to the discovery of knowledge. So, the primary aim of schooling is to serve the future i.e., to provide the students with knowledge which is related to their lives, and knowledge which they can use.

Real Love

Coming to the specifics of Real Love, some adolescents associate love with sex. Love is a very elusive reality. Love can be easily confused with infatuation and even exploitation and that brings to the question — What is real love?

Love is patient, kind, willing to excuse the faults of others; love is not jealous or boastful. Love demands commitment. Most teenagers admit that they are not ready for the kind of long term commitment that love requires in marriage.

Sex without real love will not make one happy. Without love, sex is a source of problems, worry, guilt, heartache and disappointment. If one really loves another he/she should be prepared to say NO to sex until their love is committed in marriage. Many teenagers feel that it is possible to have intercourse for keeping a relationship growing. If it is accepted, then the least option is to have "safe sex" or

Examining Pupil's Growth

Criteria	*Questions*
General Growth Objects *Personal Autonomy* (a) Selfhood (b) Individual freedom (c) Independent attitude	Does the child give any evidence of the personal autonomy as mentioned in the adjacent column?
Social Adjustment (a) Helping others (b) Sharing responsibility (c) Active participation in group discussion (d) Application of knowledge in daily life (e) Sharing with others (f) Group dynamics (g) Patience (h) Manipulation (i) Visual and auditory discrimination (j) Transformation of an abstraction into a concrete (k) Respect for sex (l) Abstinence	Does the child give any evidence of the social adjustment as mentioned in the adjacent column?
Ethical Value (a) Personal value (b) Social conscience (c) Cultural values	Does the child provide any evidence of developing ethical values mentioned in the adjacent column?
Creativity (a) Innovation (b) Discovery approach (c) Developing leisure and recreational skills	Does the child provide any evidence of creativity in the behaviour mentioned in the adjacent column?
Intellectual Capacity (a) Maximum use of all his senses (b) Development of spirit of inquiry (c) Skills of communication (d) General and specific knowledge	Does the child give any evidence of developing the intellectual capacities mentioned in the adjacent column?

"protected sex". However it is suggested to reserve sexual activity for marriage.

According to almost all religions, Hindu, Christian and other beliefs —

Abstinence is the best method to prevent AIDS among adolescents especially students.

Thus, in the curriculum the following qualities should be included that are basic elements of the perceptual field of learning.

(a) Self Experience
(b) Needs – Physical and Emotional
(c) Values (cultural, social, personal and ethical)
(d) Attitudes – Respect for fair sex, Abstinence
(e) Community and societal expectations of students

The development of curriculum must include aspects of cultural heritage so as to develop pride among pupils in their rich heritage. Students may develop an interest in learning to understand the world in which they live through an understanding of the subject matter. This can be achieved by correlating the subject matter with the cultural heritage of the students.

All these general and specific influences provide bases for a curriculum which should account for the total learning for the whole person and may encourage healthy life style among students especially for prevention of AIDS.

Curriculum Development and Evaluation in Healthy Life Style Education

Curriculum : What is it?

The term curriculum is derived from a Latin term "Currie" which means race course or body of courses etc. Webster's Third New International Dictionary defines curriculum as follows:

(i) The whole body of courses set for various majors.
(ii) Any particular body of courses set for various majors.
(iii) All planned school activities including courses of study for organized play, dramatics and clubs, etc.

The above definitions provide a traditional view of the concept of curriculum which implies that the curriculum means only the subjects taught or offered in a training course.

The following definitions of curriculum by various educators reflect the modern concept:

- Edward A. King refers the curriculum as "all means employed by the school to provide students with opportunities for desirable learning experiences". Ronald C. Doll, Havord Rugg and Hicks corroborate the above concept of curriculum.
- K.G. Saiyidain defines "curriculum as primarily an aid in the process of adjusting an individual to the

environment in which he functions from day-to-day and the wider environment in which he will have to organise his activities later".

- Alberty and Alberty refers to curriculum ". . . as the sum total of student activities which the school sponsors for the purpose of achieving its objectives".

All the above definitions of curriculum suggest that it is a total process through which an individual learns. This incorporates the 'course content' as one of its major components. However, it may be pointed out that the course content is not the curriculum – it is merely a suggested curriculum.

Kimball Wiles aptly describes the meaning of curriculum lucidly in the following manner:

> *"The word curriculum is an abstraction. It means different things to an individual, the parent, the teacher, the college professor and the lay community member. Much of the confusion is encountered when some people consider curriculum as only the formal syllabus of the school, some others visualize it as happenings in the learning situations, and some others envisage it as what happens to learners and the taught. the formal curriculum consists of the units of credit that are offered, the courses of the units of credit to students, the syllabi for these courses, the bibliographies and material used, and the evaluation devises that are selected".*

Aderson refers to curriculum ". . . as the whole of the interacting forces of total environment provided for pupils by the school and the pupils' experiences in that environment".

This definition of curriculum refers to life itself, and offers a framework of general aims and values, gives suggestions for setting learning priorities and outlines some content sequences.

Carleton Washburne defines curriculum as follows"

"... enough to include any material or activities that will effect the learning, development, attitudes, or behaviour of the individual".

This definition implies that curriculum does not depend entirely on the extrinsic constructs. But theory plays an important part in the categorization and classification process. However, the definition suggests that the curriculum must help the teacher in accounting for the following questions:

How to organize learning activities in order to produce the desirable cnvironment for optimum learning?

1. How to organize learning activities in order to produce the desirable environment for optimum learning?
2. How to utilize instructional materials to achieve the desired objective ?
3. How to evaluate an individual's performance, so as to determine the outcome of instructional material ?

The above questions are subsumed in the definition of curriculum by Gwyn, J. Minor which is as follows:

> *"The curriculum is the means for attaining the aims of philosophy of education. Being a means to the end, and not an end in itself, it usually follows and reflects educational trends and changes in the philosophy."*

E.M. Draper suggests another dimension to curriculum:

> *"The curriculum is defined today as the total learning experience which pupils have, in and out of learning institutions, under the guidance of the faculty."*

This definition widens the role of the trainer. It implies that the trainer must be aware of the many ways in which an individual learns, and the conditions, experiences and procedures that best promote learning and growth. This also implies that the teacher has training in the diagnostic and presumptive approach, experience in the individualization of instruction and a fair understanding of the continuous progress system of organization.

In other words, the teachers should be familiar with the techniques of teaching pupils to think, to create new combinations from original data; to create and develop fresh meanings and to examine various possibilities.

Summarizing the above views concerning curriculum development in sex education, one may infer that the concept of curriculum deals with the *three W's* of society,. i.e., What, Why and When ? What – What is to be taught to a learner ? It implies quantum of knowledge in sex education, with reference to societal norms and needs, to be imparted in a specific time. Why – Why is this knowledge to be given ? This suggests a rationale for imparting the quantum of knowledge, its methodology and its evaluation. When – When is this knowledge to be imparted ? This suggests a sequence of the curriculum.

Thus, curriculum in sex education can be defined as all those experiences of the individual for which an institution is responsible. It is concerned with what should be experienced. It also deals with Why, When and How a particular learning should take place and the atmosphere in which this learning occurs. The curriculum development in sex education deals with human relationships in the local environment; it refers to the values, norms and goals of the community, society and the nation.

The curriculum development in sex education should not remain theoretical and should cater to the needs related to life skills development of the students. Thus, if we want to impart meaningful sex education to adolescents in schools, to help them meet a variety of needs felt in any changing society, sex education curriculum should be related to students' problems which they have to face in the modern society with special reference to sex related issues.

Coming to the specifics of sex education, the author opines that in the first instance, the sex education instructional material may be incorporated and correlated in all the school subjects at the secondary levels. At a later stage, an independent and separate curriculum in sex education may be developed. The above approach is based on the fact that introducing sex education in schools is not favoured by some parents, community and society members. Furthermore, separate curriculum in sex education may burden the students curriculum.

Organisation of a Sex Education Programme (Course Content)

Listed below are some of the guiding principles which may be followed in the development of a sex education programme:

1. The course content should be organized into units, each of which may be related to some significant aspects of the environment, concerning sex-related matters.
2. The unit should be essentially a major problem of everyday life to which sex education may contribute an intelligent basis for human adjustment.

3. Each unit should include only a few principles of generalization in sex education instructional material.
4. The organization, in part at least, should be in the form of problems or projects to ensure education in problem solving with special reference to sex related matters.
5. The distribution of time and emphasis on various units should be determined by the total functional and social values, the "teach ability" and "learn ability", the teacher's and pupils' interest in the unit, the local significance of the unit and its value to other units of the course.
6. The organization of the course should be such that it may lead to the attainment of the immediate and ultimate objectives.

Practical Strategies for Developing a Unit

In order to develop a unit in a sex education programme, the following strategies are generally desirable:

Strategy 1

What do we want or need to do in a unit ?

This strategy involves the concept of needs assessment which may include the following items in general terms:

- What do we know ?
- What can we do ?
- What valuing experience have we had ?

To be more specific *i.e.,* in the context of sex education, the above points can be summarized as follows:

- What area or topic are you going to focus on ?

Write down students' needs that relate to the area of topic chosen concerning sex education.

Strategy 2

- What are we doing ?

This strategy involves setting of specific objectives with reference to sex education course. These objectives express the need in learning outcomes.

After setting objectives, a unit may be designed in the following manner :

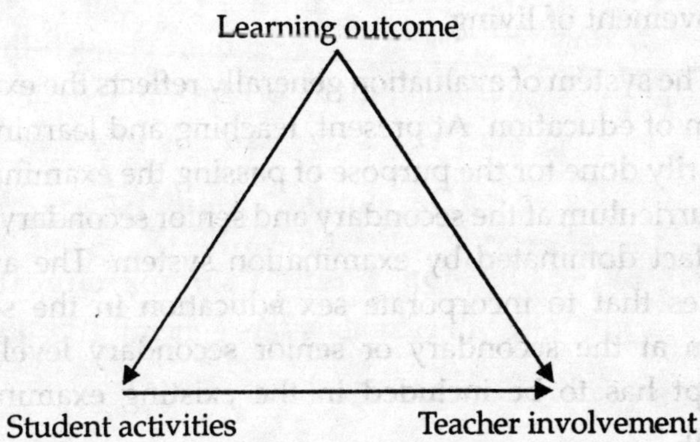

Strategy 3

How will you know when you have done it ?

Evaluation

In order to evaluate a unit, the most important point is to see whether the content in the unit satisfies the needs or meets the specific objectives.

The above discussion leads us to another aspect of curriculum development *i.e.,* Examination and Evaluation component of sex education programme.

Evaluation in Sex Education

In order to have reasonable success in imparting meaningful sex education to our adolescents in schools, a new system of evaluation is needed that will help them to acquire knowledge and life skills which will produce a better way of life for them and which will make it possible to lead the students to the discovery skills so necessary if they are to use their knowledge. The primary aim of sex education should be to serve the future, *i.e.,* to provide the students with knowledge as a usable tool for the improvement of living.

The system of evaluation generally reflects the existing system of education. At present, teaching and learning are primarily done for the purpose of passing the examination. The curriculum at the secondary and senior secondary level is in fact dominated by examination system. The author believes that to incorporate sex education in the school system at the secondary or senior secondary level, this concept has to be included in the existing examination system.

Sex education as a co-curricular subject may not be of much value as our education system, especially at the secondary and senior secondary level is geared to the examination system.

Now a question arises immediately in one's mind. What should be the nature of an evaluation/examination system in sex education if it is to promote more than memorization. The general objective of evaluation in sex education should not lay

Schematic Representation. 1

Proposed System of Evaluation in Sex Education

Student's Name ____________________ Class ________

	Unit I *E,VG, G, S, U*	*Unit II* *E,VG, G, S, U*	*Unit III* *E,VG, G, S, U*	*Unit IV* *E,VG, G, S, U*
1. General understanding of the concepts regarding sex education.				
2. Expresses ideas in terms of scientific language				
a. Observation power				
b. Forming hypotheses				
c. Drawing inferences				
d. Interpreting data				
3. Ability to express ideas clearly.				
4. Active participation in the class discussion				
5. Original approach to the course content.				
6. Home assignments.				
7. Written examination				
8. Behaviour change.				

E - Excellent (A Grade); VG - Very Good (B Grade); G - Good (B Grade); S - Satisfactory (C Grade); U - Unsatisfactory (D Grade) emphasis on accumulation of facts regarding sex but should be on development of "life skills" among adolescents at the secondary level. It should be the responsibility of the teacher, utilizing the assistance available from all sources, to determine the degree to which each student is developing his/her own life skills through scientific methods. The way in which the information regarding sex-related matters is used might vary with the purpose of the particular evaluation. That is, one purpose might be served by reporting academic information only, while for another purpose it might be of more importance to report specific skill areas such as "ability to express ideas clearly". Admittedly, this entails added work for the teacher as well as added responsibility, but the author has nowhere contended that building a system of evaluation around criteria other than academic learning should be easy. The author proposes the following system of evaluation in sex education (Schematic Representation No. 1).

To summarize, the evaluation system in sex education should be consistent with the philosophy of continuous growth. To measure progress, we must evaluate each student against himself by taking into consideration his present level and his post level of achievement as well as that of others. Thus, the evaluation system should foster development of a positive self concept for each student. Evaluation procedures must recognize the right of pupil to be appreciated for what he is and for what he has the potential to become. Evaluation in sex education should stress on teaching pupils to learn to think, to develop fresh meanings for themselves, to examine possibilities and to create new combination from original or available data. That is to say, evaluation should be itself an act of teaching.

Teaching-Learning Strategies

Sex education is a very unique aspect of human life. To transact it, one has to adopt different teaching-learning strategies. The following are some teaching-learning techniques which may be useful in actual classroom situations at the secondary and senior secondary level. These techniques provide opportunities for adolescents to inquire, share experience, ideas and discussion of attitudes, societal norms, beliefs and convictions. The key point is to develop abilities among students to make choices and decisions and take responsibilities for the same. To achieve this, these pupils at the secondary level must be clear about their own value system, to seek alternatives and be accountable for the consequences of their decisions. Thus, in sex education, the students must be encouraged to share their ideas, convictions, beliefs and experiences with their peer group regarding sex-related aspects.

The author, through his experience in Canada, U.S.A. and some other developing countries, has found that the following methods are very effective while transacting sex-related matters in the actual classroom situations especially at the secondary and senior secondary levels.

An overview of the teaching-learning strategies is available in the Schematic Representation No. 1.

Discussion Method

Open and active discussion is the keystone in imparting meaningful sex education to the adolescents. The students

Schematic Representation No. 1

An Overview Teaching Learning Strategies

						Slides, Experts Advice Column
					Fill-up the blank statement	
				Discovery Enquiry method		
			Brain storming			
		Lecture method				
	Values continuing					
Discussion (sharing of ideas, experiences)						

Audio visual method

Specialist speakers (Guest)

Popular Project method (Case-study)

Role playing

Question Cards

should be encouraged to share their myths, beliefs, ideas and experiences with the peer group (teacher as a moderator) to clarify their own values, beliefs and convictions regarding sex related issues. It may be advisable to equip the students first with the required information through films, lectures, specialist speakers and reading assignments.

This method can be effective in the following manner:

Small Groups ("Buzz Groups")

This may consist of three to five students. Selection of these students may be done by draw of lots. The teacher's role is to guide the discussion on a specific sex related issue and it may be followed by a worksheet. A representative from the group may be nominated so as to report the proceedings and outcomes of the discussion to the class and the teacher.

Medium Size Group (Circular Group Discussions)

This consists of six to ten students. The discussion takes place in a systematic manner around the circle. Every student may be encouraged to participate but may not be forced to participate.

Large Group Discussion (Class Discussion)

Small Group (Buzz Groups), and Medium Size Group (Circular Groups) may be asked to assemble together for a joint discussion regarding sex related issues which they have discussed in their respective groups and make provision for any additional comments which any student wants to make regarding the above discussion. The emphasis is on group and dynamics, interaction, with some tangible outcome.

Values Continuum

Value continuum method of transacting sex education in schools is quite relevant and appropriate as it encourages students to assess their own value system, attitudes, beliefs and convictions regarding sex related issues and matters. In this method, the students are asked to take stand regarding their personal convictions about sex in a classroom. The teacher may draw a line on the blackboard giving two extremes :

Girls are more serious ________________ Boys are more serious
in studies in studies.

This values continuum has been discussed in the preceding chapter entitled, "Sex Education and Values Clarification".

Lecture Method

It is one of the oldest and most commonly used methods in most of our schools. In this method, the students are passive listeners and play an active role in learning. Lecture method has some merits such as it is a less time consuming method and is quite relevant for a large group of students at a time. For a special lecture on sex related matters, it may be quite useful. But the students may be encouraged to ask questions during the lecture. It may include use of visual aids, slides, anatomical drawings followed by 'group activities'. This lecture method may provide adequate information about sex-related issues and encourage the students to ask questions.

Brain Storming

This is a psychological sound technique which encourages students to be creative and express their beliefs, experiences, ideas and convictions regarding sex issues in a frank manner and try to find the solution for the same by using alternate solutions technique. This involves other methods such as discussion, lecture and role-play etc. All ideas and views expressed by the students in this brain storming session are to be appreciated. Adequate time (10 minutes) may be allotted to generate and think about ideas. It is sometimes used as a warm up activity which may lead to a serious discussion on another related sex issue.

Discovery/Enquiry Method

It is a psychological fact that as compared to acquiring knowledge or information from others, it is more efficacious to acquire the same through personal effort by probing or discovering. This method is quite apt for imparting meaningful sex education in schools. Students may be encouraged to bring clipping from the newspapers regarding sex-related issues. These may be discussed in a classroom.

The principles underlying this method of teaching-learning are as follows:

(i) The principle of activity.
(ii) The principle of logical thinking
(iii) The principle of purposeful experience
(iv) The principle of mental development.

This method is based on self-study. The educative process in this method consists of the following:

(i) Presentation of the problem.
(ii) Direction and guidance – Helpful direction and guidance is given to the students at first.
(iii) Arriving at hypothesis followed by its verification and testing.
(iv) Observation and tabulation of facts.
(v) Generalization and application.

The teacher's role in this method is to act as a good guide. He should possess good insight.

Enquiry approach encourages students to think scientifically and develop independent thinking. It lays greater emphasis on self-education. It generates self-confidence and self-reliance in students and motivates them to think and understand. The teacher and students have to be active in this method. If properly implemented, it is a unique teaching-learning strategy especially dealing with sex related issues.

Fill-up the Blank Statements

The teacher is required to have fill up the blank sentences regarding sex related issues. For example, Love without sex.

The students are asked to complete the sentences anonymously. This may be done by the teacher on the blackboard as a warming strategy for discussion. This may also be done in a group work.

Expert's Advice Column

This advice column technique is quite prevalent in the West especially dealing with sex related issue. The students may bring "real life" problems regarding sex related issues and the same may be sent to expert (or a teacher) for his/her advice. The response of the real life problem may be discussed in classroom (small groups). These small groups may bring their comments/observations on the above problem and discuss it in a classroom.

Audio-Visual Aids Method

Audio-visual aids (films, film-strip, radio, posters, etc.) supported/based teaching learning strategy is quite effective in discussing sex related issues. The teacher's role in this method is quite crucial especially in the context of selection of audio-visual material (film) which is appropriate and relevant to the age group. The film/audio must fulfill the objectives of the sex related issues. The film should be interesting, stimulating and may present various views on debatable issues concerning sex related matters. The students may be asked to note salient features in the film which may be taken as topics for discussion. Before presenting the audio-visual material to the students, the teacher must have a pre-view of this material. The content in this approach must be factually correct, up-to-date, interesting and relevant. Audio-visual technique is a supplementary method of teaching-learning and may not be a substitute for other methodology of teaching-learning (books, lectures, inquiry approach, role-playing etc.)

Specialist Speaker

In the opinion of the author, this is the most effective strategy for imparting meaningful sex education instructions to the adolescents. It is generally realized that teachers and students do not feel comfortable in discussing sex related matters. Some teachers, especially female teachers, are hesitant to discuss the sex-related concepts such as masturbation, nightfall and other biological issues. Thus, guest lectures, especially delivered experts, may be quite ineffective strategy but the following aspects may be taken into consideration before having expert guest speakers.

(i) Purpose of the topic for discussion.
(ii) Presentation of several points of view on the controversial sex related issues.
(iii) Length, date, time of the lecture.
(iv) Encouraging students to ask questions. They may prepare a list of questions before the lecture.
(v) Panel of expert speakers based on their expertise and their ability to lecture or make presentation in an interesting manner.
(vi) Panel may include doctors, health-care personnel, social scientists, sex counsellors.
(vii) Follow-up discussions regarding the lectures.

Project Method — Case-Study

Project method may be based on the real life situational study-case. The project may focus on prejudices, beliefs, attitudes and conviction on sex related issues. The topics of the project may be appropriate to the age-group.

The philosophical basis of this method is pragmatism and is propounded by William Kilpatrick. Kilpatrick, Stevenson and Parket were the chief 'proponents' of this method and defined it as follows:

Kilpatrick : A Project is a whole-hearted purposeful activity proceeding in a social environment.

Stevenson : A Project is a problematic act caused to conclusion in its natural setting.

Parket : A Project is a unit of activity in which pupils are made responsible for planning and carrying out work as per plan.

The project method is a purposeful activity which is carried out by the pupils in natural environment. More emphasis is given on creativity. The following principles are utilized in this method:

(a) Principle of reality and utility
(b) Principle of learning by experience.

The following are the steps in this method:

(i) Choosing the problem; case-study and project planning;
(ii) Planning
(iii) Carrying out the project (case-study)
(iv) Evaluation of the project.

Students are active participants as they are involved in purposeful activity. Many opportunities for developing individual skills are existent. This method develops self-confidence and self-reliance among the students. Learning is not bookish but related to life. It is a psychological method since learning takes place through experiences. This method encourages students to explore and to endeavour to make inquiries and fosters development of sociability and cooperation since several students are simultaneously engaged in carrying the project/case study successfully.

This teaching/learning strategy is quite effective in transacting sex education related matters.

Role Playing

This is another strategy for imparting meaningful sex education in schools. The objective of this strategy is to have the experience of the character whom they portray. The other class-fellows are required to observe and analyze the character's role in a meaningful manner.

Role playing is not to be taken as a form of entertainment activity. Open-ended situations involving emotions are encouraged in this activity. Role players should be given roles to be portrayed on voluntary basis taking into account the suitability aspect, and should be given adequate time before the beginning of the role-play activity. The time limit and setting of the stage should be carefully planned. Discussion should be followed by role-play activity.

This teaching learning strategies, if not planned carefully, may not be successful. The guidelines suggested above are to be taken into consideration before implementing this strategy in dealing with sex related issues.

Question Cards

The teacher may develop question items concerning sex education related issues. The students are asked to write the answers on these cards. The answer-cards from different students are collected and discussed in a class. In this activity, each student is an active participant. The question-items may *inter alia* include definition of "love", and "sex". It may include items concerning pros and cons of premarital sex, importance of love, affection, loyalty and honesty in a sexual relationship.

Popular Songs, Poems (Music)

The teacher may play the music or lyrics which may have feeling of love and sex. This may include radio music. The students may be encouraged to collect the lyrics for discussion depicting love related issues. The lyrics and songs may be discussed.

Reference

Steven Bignel : *Sex Education Teachers Guide andResource Manual* California: Network Publication, 1982

8

Teaching Healthy Life Style

We are all aware that one of the most frequent modes of transmission of HIV/AIDS virus is through sexual contact. Unlike other STDs (Sexually Transmitted Diseases) like Gonorrhea, syphilis, Genital Sores, Genital warts, Herpes etc., AIDS virus is incurable because up till now the HIV infection that leads to AIDS cannot be cured. Prevention and caution in sexual relations are the only means to combat this killer disease. It is, therefore, imperative to impart meaningful sex education or sexual health learning in our schools with special reference to our cultural and societal norms. To discuss the concept of sexual health, it may be desirable to define this term.

Sexual Health – What is it?

The World Health Organization (WHO) defines the term as follows:

> *"The integration of physical, emotional, intellectual and social aspects of sexuality in a way that positively enriches and promotes personality, communication and love".*

Thus, sexual health is not confined to sexual intercourse but it lays emphasis on the positive expression of a person's sexuality which includes self-esteem, body image, social roles and relationships with others. Sexual health also takes into consideration the constraints and the freedoms about sex education in the respective cultures.

Sexual Health in Schools

It is an admitted fact that we are all sexual beings from the day of our birth till our doom's day. It is an integral part of our life and cannot be denied. Our social fabric and cultural heritage affects the degree to which we can talk about sexuality. In different cultures, the sexuality may be discussed freely in terms of heterosexuality (male/female sexual relationships), celibacy 'no sexual relations', and homo-sexuality (sexual relations with those of the same sex). The major events in the sexual learning, such as puberty, menopause, marriage and childbirth need adequate discussion in the schools. Furthermore, it may also be desirable to debate upon the physical/emotional changes which take place at the adolescent stage.

Physical/Emotional Changes in Adolescence

The World Health Organization defines "adolescents" as being between the ages of 10 and 24. This is an age in which a person matures physically, psychologically and socially from childhood to adulthood (WHO 1989). Physical change in this period is called "Puberty".

Physical Changes in Adolescents

Boys	*Girls*
- Voice Change	- Growth in height, breasts and underarm hair
- Growth in sexual organs and height	- Growth in sexual organs
- Penile erection	- Production of ova
	- Menstruation

Emotional Changes

These need support to deal with emotions and feelings about sexual attraction and orientation. These changes will also depend on cultural values, attitudes, customs and accepted societal norms.

Schematic Representation No. 1

Sexual Health and Life Cycle

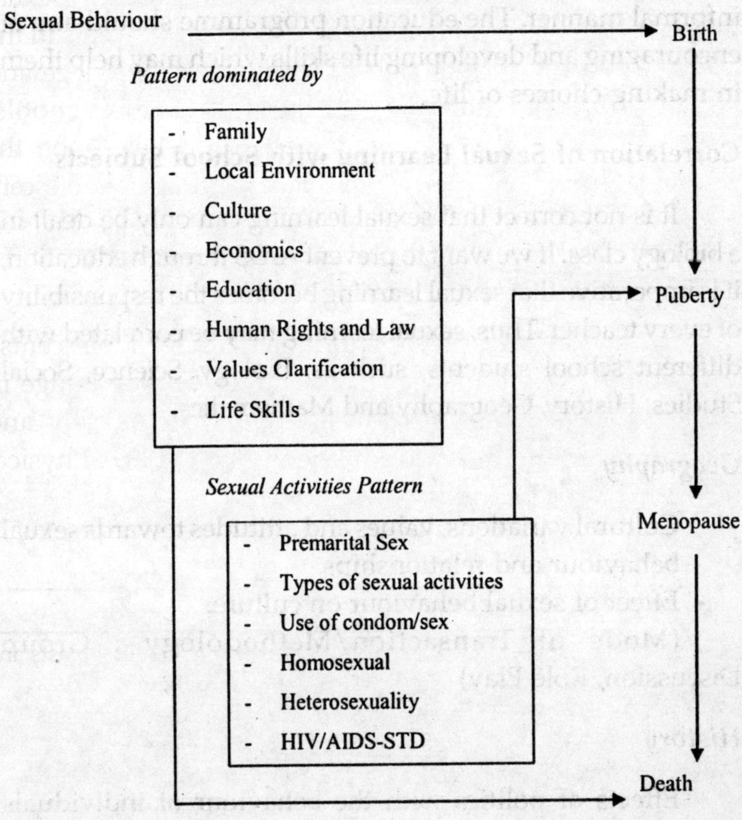

Source : Adapted from Introduction to Sexual Health, Red Cross Societies, Geneva. Sexual Health and Life Cycle. (Sexual health includes thoughts, emotions and self esteem)

The above mentioned changes in adolescents can be aptly described in the Schematic Representation No. 1.

Talking About Healthy Life Style in Indian Schools

In our culture, it may not be very acceptable to talk about sex outside the confines of marriage especially in schools. But it may be possible to discuss about sexual health within the educational programmes in formal and informal manner. The education programme should aim at encouraging and developing life skills which may help them in making choices of life.

Correlation of Sexual Learning with School Subjects

It is not correct that sexual learning can only be dealt in a biology class. If we want to prevent AIDS through education, it is imperative that sexual learning becomes the responsibility of every teacher. Thus, sexual learning may be correlated with different school students, such as, Biology, Science, Social Studies, History, Geography and Mathematics.

Geography

- Cultural variations, values and attitudes towards sexual behaviour and relationships.
- Effect of sexual behaviour on culture.

(Mode of Transaction/Methodology : Group Discussion, Role Play)

History

Effects of politics with the behaviour of individuals and peoples conflicts and peace between individuals and people over sexual patterns.

(Mode of Transaction/Methodology : Observation, discussion and debates)

Sociology

- Impact of sexual behaviour on life style
- Effect of family and culture on life style
- Effect of sexual behaviour on social behaviour

(Mode of Transaction/Methodology : Discussion, Role play and Research)

Mathematics

- Epidemiology of AIDS/HIV infection
- Health for All and its effect on Economics

(Mode of Transaction/Methodology :Working with Experts)

Biology

- Human Reproductive System
- AIDS and STDs
- Prevention of AIDS and STDs
- Pregnancy and Birth
- Hormone change at puberty
- Functions of immune system at cellular level

(Mode of Transaction/Methodology :Building models of cell construction, Group discussion, Visits to health centres)

Science

- Composition of body
- Food
- Balanced diet
- Good living habits
- AIDS primary messages

(Mode of Transaction/Methodology: Observation/ Discussion, Role play, Community health fair)

The above correlation to Sexual Health with different school subjects suggests that this subject is not only to be dealt by the biology or science teacher alone. It is the responsibility of all teachers at the secondary level to integrate sexual health learning with all school subjects in a natural manner.

In addition to the above, the following basic knowledge about Sexually Transmitted Diseases may be given to all students at the secondary level in simplistic manner.

Basic Information about STDs (Sexually Transmitted Diseases)

Sexually transmitted diseases are infections transmitted or passed on from one individual to another by sexual intercourse. The most common diseases are :

1. ***Gonorrhea***
   Symptoms : A yellow/green discharge and pain during urination. In females, there may by no symptoms at all.
   Treatment : As advised by the doctor; antibiotic.
2. ***Syphilis***
   Symptoms : A small, painless ulcer on the genitals that disappears gradually. A red rash may occur over the body. The last stage of syphilis may lead to insanity, paralysis and death.
   Treatment : As advised by the doctor, antibiotic.
3. ***Genital Sores***
   Symptoms : Painful and frequently infected sores on the genitals.
   Treatment : As advised by the doctor, antibiotics.
4. ***Genital Warts***
   Symptoms : Similar to Warts. Small hard lumps appear on the genitals.
   Treatment : A wart removing preparation is applied to each wart.

5. ***Herpes***

Symptoms : It is characterized by painful grouped vesicles which occur around the mouth or genitals. This may be accompanied by aches, pains, swollen glands and high fevers..

Treatment : Can be treated but can not be completely cured.

Recurrence is very common – Doctor's advice is mandatory.

Integrated Approach to Healthy Life Style Education Instructions

As mentioned earlier, sex education instructions are not to be dealt in the biology classes. It is the responsibility of all secondary and senior secondary teachers to correlate the aspect of sex education/life skills education with the other school subjects. To achieve this objective, it may be imperative to utilize integrated approach to sex education instructions at the secondary and senior secondary levels.

To exemplify the above approach, a few specific concepts in different school subjects at the secondary level have been given.

The given examples are merely suggestive. The teacher has to structure the content and extent of the topic keeping in view the family background of the children and the society they come from.

Correlation with School Subjects

Correlating 'Sex Education' with Literature (English Language) Social and Ethical Values.

Suggested Activity

Male and female role and language

Objective: To help students recognise roles.

Correlating 'Sex Education' with Biology

Contents	*Explanations Examples*	*Activity — Question-Answer Session*
All systems of human body	Internal organs to be explained with the help of charts.	Questions about gender differences in plants, animals – Nature's way of providing pysical features in all living things for propagation reproduction.
Differences between male and female growth.	Discuss mammals and their special features, functions – behaviour.	Questions like why in most species female have a different role to play. Evaluation can be done by holding a science quiz.
Difference between egg-laying animals and mammals that have babies.	Male – female birds and their behaviour.	
	• The physical changes that take place between the age of twelve and sixteen.	The students should be encouraged to discuss the personal experience of those changes.
	• The emotional trauma through which the children of this age pass.	Discussions should be encouraged in the class. The physical changes e.g., growth of beard, change of voice in case of boys can be demonstrated in the class.
	• Hormonal changes which take place inside the body leading to the growth of secondary sex organs.	Pictures showing dwarfism and gigantism indicating hormonal imbalances.
	To explain that growth is a natural phenomenon.	Discussion on certain abnormal features which result due to abnormal development

Contents	*Explanations Examples*	*Activity — Question-Answer Session*
Reproductive systems:	Differentiate reproductive system in human body.	The students should collect details of different methods of reproduction.
	Significance of sex organs in case of sexual reproduction involving intimate contact of male and female in all living organisms.	The students should visit agriculture farms to observe various methods of sexual reproduction in case of plant.
		The students can observe the pollen grain under a microscope to understand that the pollen grains (male cells) are transferred from male flowers to female flowers for fertilization.
		To study sexual reproduction in rabbits, frogs, etc.
		Evaluation: The students should record their observations in the note books and discuss in the class.
Fertilization:	Fertilization involving fusion of male and female gamete.	Charts can be shown to the students about the structure of sperm and an egg.
External and Internal Fertilisation.	Differentiations between a sperm and an egg.	Discussions about the animals in case where development of fetus takes place inside the mother and those animals where development takes place outside mother's body.
	Formation of Zygote.	

Contents	*Explanations Examples*	*Activity — Question-Answer Session*
	Development of foetus inside the mother's womb.	The students can be asked to visit a nearby pond and observe the development of fertilized egg of frog. (External fertilization).
	In case of internal fertilization, examples of dogs, cats, cows, can be quoted with special emphasis on human beings.	Group discussion may be encouraged to clear the difference between external and internal fertilization.]
Pregnancy:	Fusion of male and female gamete forms zygote which is the start of pregnancy. Importance of umbilical cord can clear doubts about belly button.	Various stages of development of zygote may be discussed. The students may be asked to record in their note books various embryonic stages of multi-cellular animals.
Menstruation Cycle:	Menstruation cycle and its role in pregnancy. Maintenance of personal hygiene.	If necessary, separate classes may be taken for girls to brief them about the monthly periods. They should discuss the doubts.
	Fears or superstition about menstruation may be discussed. and cleared. To clarify that menstruation is simply a base aspect of being a woman.	Teachers should clearly explain various problems which are faced by girls during menstruation period.

Contents	*Explanations Examples*	*Activity — Question-Answer Session*
	Preparation of questionnaire containing questions which may arise in minds of youngsters.	Teachers can act as a counsellor and encourage the students to discuss freely the problems, if any, faced by them during menstruation period.
	Links of menstruation with pregnancy can be explained by using charts.	Because of taboo, children may not be able to discuss problems freely, the teacher can prepare a set of questionnaire regarding menstruation cycle and other related problems. The teacher after answering the questionnaires can ask the students to discuss the problems in the class.
Contents Semen and sperms:	Urinogenital system in case of males may be explained in detail. More emphasis should be given to comprehension rather than memorization.	The students should be able to differentiate between urine and sperm since there is a common passage for the exit of urine and sperms.
		Students should be asked to draw diagrams showing urinogenital system. Discussion showing urinogenital systems can also help them understand clearly the link between urinary system and reproductive system in case of male.

Contents	*Explanations Examples*	*Activity — Question-Answer Session*
Contents: Artificial insemination.	Importance of artificial insemination in case of animals. Benefits of cross-breeding.	The students can be asked to visit a veterinary centre for collecting data about artificial insemination in case of buffaloes, cows, etc. They should also get details of high yielding varieties of animals and crops. **Evaluation**: Questions can be put up by the teacher in the class. List the contributions made by scientists for improvement of crops by crossbreeding.
Contents Wet dreaming	Wet dreams or seminal emissions that occur during night. Day-dreaming.	The teacher can prepare a questionnaire regarding problems faced by the pre-adolescent age-group boys. The questionnaires should cover all the problems related to wet dreams and seminal emissions. Boys should be encouraged to come out with their feelings so that they are guided properly. They should be taught that the emissions are normal.

Contents	*Explanations Examples*	*Activity — Question-Answer Session*
		Healthy discussions can clear the doubts about masturbation.
Contents Mitosis, Meiosis	Importance of chromosomes. Resemblance of off-springs to the parents. Heredity and inheritance of genes.	The group discussion can encourage a student to reason out as to how various genetic characteristics are inherited.
Communicable Diseases	Sexual diseases like syphilis, gonorrhea AIDS, etc.	To note the various diseases which spread by communication.
	To discuss the structure of RNA and DNA.	To visit the health centres and collect the data of patients suffering from AIDS.
	Transfer of HIV through seminal fluids and blood during intimate contact.	To discuss the reasons of spread of AIDS. Discuss the importance of marriage. Group discussions about the precaution taken for the prevention of AIDS. Disadvantages of free sex.

Contents	*Explanations Examples*	*Activity — Question-Answer Session*
Family Planning	Benefits of small family.	The students should be asked to collect the data from family welfare centres about steps taken by them to control population.
	Population problems.	
	Use of contraceptives.	The students can be asked to note down the benefits of small family and dangers of unchecked growth of world population. Charts can be used showing vasectomy in males, tubectomy in case of females.
		Group discussions can be encouraged.

Procedure

(i) Giving the students a list of word pairs having both masculine and feminine words.
(ii) Dividing into groups.
(iii) Asking the students to explain and discuss implications of each word.
(iv) How is masculine word different from feminine word; for example Patron and Matron, Sir and Madam.
(v) Discuss whether our sex is more dominant than that of the others; Chairman, Mankind, Foreman.
(vi) Should there be a change in social set up.

Suggested Activity

Writing Composition on Imageries

Objective -To help the students to clarify their concepts about male and female roles.

Procedure:

(i) Giving opposite topics to opposite sex: For example: To the boys.
Giving a topic like –
If I were a princess, or if I were the headmistress of my school.
If I were the heroine of a film.
To the Girls
If I were the night watchman
If I were the headman of my family.
(ii) Asking the girl students what they are not allowed to do ?
(iii) What are the things which the boys must not do ?

Suggested Activity

Adjectives and Related Sex

Procedure:

(i) Give a list of adjectives applied to both male and female.

(ii) Ask the students to draw two columns male and female. Write the appropriate adjective in the relevant column.

(iii) Why a particular adjective was written in a particular column ?

(iv) Ask the students if any of the girls have 'masculine' qualities such as a tall girl or any of the boys have a feminine qualities, such as a tender boy. What difficulties have they to face due to these qualities.

Suggested Activity

Puzzles

Objective

To find out solutions to the problems on the basis of students' assumptions about male or female roles.

Procedure

The study containing problems may be got Xeroxed and distributed among students. Ask them to read and write solutions.

Suggested Activity

Male and Female Role and Literature

Importance of Being Earnest Play (X)

Objective

Discussion on male and female roles.

Procedure

1. Ask the students to read the script.
2. Distribute roles among the students.
3. Ask the students to enact.
4. Ask questions:
   (i) Do the roles of female characters appear realistic ?
   (ii) Do the characters fulfill your expectations in terms of what you feel a man should be ?
   (iii) Are you influenced by the lady character? Does she behave as a woman should ?
   (iv) How does the play affect your opinion about men and women?

Suggested Activity

Fiction

Health (x)

Objective

Making them aware of STD diseases.

Procedure

1. Listening to an interview of a doctor.
2. Making notes while listening.
3. Giving sheets containing tables to the students such as:

AIDS VIRUS ...	Infectious agent
Treatment	—
After-effects/side effects.	—
Suggestions to prevent	—

4. Ask the students to complete the table on the basis of note.

Suggested Activity

Comparison of different cultures stories from different societies

Sex Education and Teaching of Hindi

Correlating Sex Education with the Local Language
For example: Teaching of Hindi in India

S.No	*Chapter*	*Area to be correlated*	*Activities*
I	Teaching of *Rasas* with specific reference to *Shringar* Ras (which is related with the feeling of love and sex).	1. Natural instinct. 2. Importance of love and sex. 3. Behavioural aspects of adolescents. 4. Healthy sex and sublimation of emotions.	1. Ask the students to name the feelings and emotions which they experience. 2. Various forms of love; list them – Prem, Shradha).
II.	Teaching of play - *'Tootte Parivesh'* by Vishnu Prabhakar (The play deals with the problems of a family of eight members (three sons, three daughters, and parents), in specific but points towards the problems of today's society. The struggle between the old and younger generation and its effects.	1. Emotional problems of an adolescent. 2. Taboos of society. 3. Importance of the institution of marriage. 4. Free sex with reference to society like ours, the dis-advantages, STD. 5. Discussion of behaviour of characters like – Vivek, Deepti, Zarina.	1. Discuss with the students their behavioural changes and reasons thereof. 2. Encourage them to come out with their independent views about life. 3. Discussion on the issue – 'Importance of institution of marriage.'

S.No	Chapter	Area to be correlated	Activities
III.	Teaching of poetry *'Reeti Kal'* (Bihari, Padmakar, Gyana Nand).	1. Day dreams and how to control them. 2. Explanation of dreams with reference to sub-conscious and unconscious. 3. Healthy attitude towards other sex.	1. Class discussion. 2. Paragraph writing. 3. Importance of dreams.
IV.	Teaching of Novel: (*Rani Laxmi Bai*) (Class – XII).	1. Discussion of ills of extra-marital relations (with reference to the previous and present time). 2. Had there been no *'Ali Bahadur'* (illegitimate son of king Radhunath Rao), the scenario of struggle for independence (1857) would have changed.	Group discussion – 1. My family. 2. The difference between a home and a house.
V.	Works of 'Jai Shankar Prasad'. (a) Kamayani. (b) Dhruv Swamini. (c) Story : Gunda Puruskar (Classes XI and XII).	1. The changing status of woman in our society. 2. Role of men and women. 3. Respect towards opposite sex. 4. Strengthening of institution of marriage 5. Role of teenagers. 6. Prostitution – an ugly spot on our society.	Paragraph writing: (a) Indian woman. (b) Ours is a male-dominated society. (c) Had I been a boy. (d) Had I been a girl.

S.No	*Chapter*	*Area to be correlated*	*Activities*
VI.	Poetic work of 'Hari Vansh Rai Bachchan'. (a) *Pati Ki Pehchan..* (b) *Tum Mujhe Pukaro.* (c) *Yug Ke Yuva.* (d) *Madhu Bala, Mad-hushala, Madhukalash.* (e) Story : *Gunda Puruskar* (Classes XI and XII)	1. Adolescents and their world of imagination.. 2. To make the student familiar with the hard realities of life. 3. To develop realistic attitude.	Group discussion -: Dream versus Realities
VII.	Teaching of prose: (a) Essay – *Burf Aur Dhoop* (Vidya Niwas Mishra). (b) *Seep aur Chanda* (Vidya Niwas Mishra). (c) *Nai Sanskriti Ki Ore* – Ram Vriksha Benipuri. (d) *Jeene ki Kala* (Mahadevi Verma).	1. To explain the meaning of culture. 2. Salient features of our culture. 3. Invasion of western culture on our culture – drug mania, sex mania. 4. Real happiness lies in the sublimation of instincts. 5. Free sex leads to frustration, humi-liation and diseases like AIDS, HERPES, 6. To motivate students not to follow West blindly but to strengthen our own culture.	To collect literature related to AIDS (from newspapers, magazines) and prepare a magazine.

S.No	Chapter	Area to be correlated	Activities
VIII.	Essay writing: (a) Teenagers of today. (b) Our national problems. (c) Population control. (d) Changing values and Indian society. (e) Invasion of Western culture. (f) Home, happy home. (g) Dreaded disease – AIDS.	1. To make the students aware of the problems of our society. 2. To impart knowledge about healthy sex and population control. 3. To help them to think independently.	Slogan writing competition
IX.	Letter writing : Letters to: (a) Editor; (b) Friends; (d) Younger brothers, and sisters on the above mentioned topics for essay writing.	1 To enable the students to have healthy attitude towards sex. 2 To encourage them to come out with their problems. 3 To inculcate healthy reading habits. 4 To enable the students to have scientific attitude towards sex instead of getting information from cheap literature. 5 To emphasize the importance of personal hygiene and to caution the students against quacks.	Suggesting names of good books, novels, scientifically written books on sex, adolescents, personal hygiene etc.

Objective

Teaching ethical values

Procedure

(i) Collect stories of different societies displaying opposite ethical values.
(ii) Ask the students to go through them.
(iii) Ask them to fit one story related to one society into the texture of the other.
(iv) Discuss the reactions.
(v) Which aspects will not be acceptable in which societies and why ?

Sex Education and Social Sciences

Correlating Sex Education with Social Sciences

Correlation of Sex education with Social Studies/Social Sciences cannot be over-emphasized. Practical activities and correlation with values clarifications have been discussed in detail separately. However, the Social Studies teacher may lay emphasis on social, moral and ethical aspect of sex education/instructions. The teacher may discuss sex and related issues such as gender bias, sex exploitation and AIDS in an open and frank discussion with students.

To sum up, the above mentioned are a few examples of correlation of sex education with the school subjects at the secondary and senior secondary levels. The teacher may develop his study units regarding sex education and correlate them with the concepts of school subjects at the secondary level. The teacher is the ultimate person who has to transact this knowledge.

10

Awareness and Involvement of Community

(Introducing Healthy Life Style Education in Rural Schools)

Majority of the third world countries are primarily lands of villages with people of various faiths. Majority of population in these countries live in rural areas. However, most of the recent educational movements have centred around the need of cities and urban schools, overlooking the special needs of the rural people.

We are aware that the killer disease AIDS is attacking the third world countries in a big way, especially in rural and remote areas. This may affect adolescent pupils who become sexually active especially in these areas. It may also affect adolescents who are victims of social evils like drug addiction (due to various reasons such as inability to cope with heavy school curriculum load, lack of meaningful education, poverty, frustration and absence of proper role models).

What are today's students in rural high schools supposed to learn ? What are they learning actually ? A study of high school subjects contribute to anything else besides facts, concepts and generalizations ? Any skills ? Any values ? Any hope for the future?

One does not have to study the pattern of high school management in rural third world to realize the need for reconstruction of curriculum in order to play a constructive role. The curriculum should help the pupils to become conversant with their day-to-day problems and train them in finding solutions when they become alert citizens.

The present weakness in our school system is that it is not looked upon as an institution. It is considered something remote, although useful. Few people know how to reform the ailment. One of the burning issues in education is how the people should be mobilized in the education of school-going adolescents so that they do not become dropouts, get frustrated with lack of job opportunities and become victim of alcohol, drug abuse and AIDS,

To overcome these problems, especially of AIDS, importance of sex education in schools cannot be over emphasized. As mentioned earlier, introduction of sex education in schools is a Herculean task as "sex" is considered "taboo" which is not to be discussed with adolescents. Thus, to prevent AIDS through sex education, it is imperative to seek cooperation from the community.

The author opines that without awareness and involvement drive regarding prevention of AIDS among adolescents through sex education in schools, the prevention of this killer disease through education would be a wishful thinking without any purposive outcome. Thus, awareness drive regarding importance and necessity of sex education in schools (with special reference to culture, social and moral values of the third world) may be initiated in a meaningful manner. Orientation programmes regarding prevention of AIDS through sex education for parents and community members may be organized. Exhibitions, folk dreams and street plays may be organized. Unless the parents and community are convinced, motivated and involved in introduction of "Sex Education in Schools", especially for prevention of AIDS, sex education in schools in Asia would be a futile exercise. Role of media in this effort cannot be over-emphasized.

Furthermore, it is gratifying to note a meaningful role to be played by Panchayat in education processes in the third world, especially India. To deliberate upon the role of community in sex education in schools, it is necessary to discuss the term "community power".

Role of Community Power Structure

Community Power is the ability of individuals or groups to determine the behaviour of others, against their wishes. The structure of power within a community refers to the relationship between individuals and groups holding power.

The network of this relationship determines what is called the Politics of Education which, in turn, proves often to the chagrin of educationists, a most potent influence in education decision making. In a way, it brings sudden and major educational changes which necessarily have to be tailored to the local and real even of parochial needs. The diversification, which caters to various interests, ensures cooperation from the people who matter. Community power structure refers to power relations or patterns of influence in the community which may be having influence on the school or sometimes only in an advisory capacity. Influencing change in the rural high school through the community power structure itself is sometimes a difficult undertaking, but recent studies suggest it is not an impossible one. The school system is a sub-system of the community power structure. There exists a line of communication between the school system and the community structure. Officials of the State Department of Education, school administrators and teachers must initiate and influence changes through the community power structure in India.

Strategies for Change

For desired education changes with the initiation of prevention of AIDS through sex education programme, professionals and local community leaders need to develop appropriate strategies in the prevailing power structure, which will :

(i) promote adoption of power structure through mobilization of community services, local advisory committees and the existing political structure in a community; and

(ii) produce an appreciable change to make it open to radical educational reforms.

In rural third world, this can be materialized by utilization of the services of local advisory committees and the village political structure.

Local community resource groups may comprise individuals and organizations in the village who want to help in the prevention of AIDS through introduction of sex education programmes in the secondary schools of their community. These committees might include retired teachers, civil servants, professionals and people who are, directly or indirectly, as officials or parents, concerned with and/or interested in prevention of AIDS through sex education in schools. This approach will ensure public involvement in the schools and the establishment of community schools.

Local Advisory Committee(LAC)

It would be worthwhile to deliberate upon the term 'Local Advisory Committees' which may be conceived as a group of local community people whose function is to advise the State Departments of Education in the third world countries regarding curricular or non-curricular school matters, especially those relating to prevention of AIDS programmes, with special reference to sex education in the context of cultural heritage of third world countries. This will facilitate that the local advisory committees have a wholesome impact on educational concerns of the community, with special reference to prevention of AIDS among school adolescent pupils. Through sex education, it is necessary to specify their advantages, organization, functions, and intent in school matters (especially those relating to sex education at the high school level).

Advantages of LAC

(1) It enhances public awareness of the school system, its problems and issues especially those relating to prevention of AIDS through sex education among High School pupils.
(2) It improves the quality and relevance of education to the community.
(3) It transforms schools into miniature communities.
(4) It brings the school out of its isolation and dovetails with important aspects of community life.
(5) It provides climate which facilitates educational innovations in the school system with specific reference to preventing AIDS at the high school level through imparting sex education with reference to cultural, social, moral and ethical values.

The impression that the present day Asian society is dormant, static and impervious to social, economic and scientific changes is highly misleading. In spite of illiteracy in the third world, people have the wisdom of ages. They are cautious and not dazzled by appearances. Despite their well-tried, time-honoured, even primitive way of doing things, they will make sure that the new ways will work. The society is not quiescent, but it is the concern for security which determines the attitudinal change. They all want modern education for their wards; for them modern means something new, relevant, meaningful, problem-solving and not merely novel in usage.

If we want to impart meaningful sex education to school adolescent pupils, especially in rural areas, to prevent AIDS and help them meet their felt needs, the school system should seek the opinion of community members to win their support for enriching the quality of educational services. This approach increases public understanding of the school and also improves the quality and relevance of education to the community in general.

If school curriculum remains as theoretical as it is and does not cater to the needs of the local community, it will fail to get any support from the community. This conviction leads us to suggest that our first step should be; "transform schools into miniature communities". This can be accomplished effectively by utilization of local community resource groups or local advisory groups. In this connection, state departments of education, school administrators and teachers have civic responsibilities along with other citizens to harness the existing power. This may also help in prevention of AIDS through sex education instructions in schools. Education development in traditional societies often disturbs the existing power structure materially and the relationship between the haves and the have-nots. This may be starting point of a controversy. If the existing power structure is not amenable to influence, guidance, prodding, or persuasion, etc., what other means should be employed to remove the perpetual indifference or resistance to change? Obviously, with existing political system, the decisive factors have to be enlightened resulting in political maturity of the people, the quality of leadership, the economic conditions, and social harmony and persuasion of local community to see importance of sex education in prevention of AIDS in the schools.

Purpose of LACs

Local Advisory Committees are established primarily to assist the Departments of Education in gathering relevant information from parents pertaining to sex education in schools. Their role in the community services should be of an advisory nature rather than of decision making. Their purpose is to assist the school and department officials in the local school decision making processes. The meaning of "advisory" should be made very clear to the local advisory committee in order to avoid any possible future conflict over their magnitude of influence and power. This approach should form the relationship among the department education officials, principals, headmasters, teachers and other citizens in the community.

In order to prevent any misunderstanding, it would be advisable for the department of education to make a statement of policy regarding the "power" and "advisory" nature of the local advisory committee. The following information should be included in the statement:

- Purpose of the committee.
- Size of the committee (number of members).
- Duration.
- Mode of selection of members.
- Mode of replacement of members whose term expires.

- Method of communication between the local advisory committee and the department of education regarding introduction of sex education in schools..
- Transaction of sex education instructional material worth reference to societal cultural heritage.
- Evaluation of the effectiveness of the committee.
- Needless to say, such committees will neither function identically nor would they have similar influence. One of the advisory committees may deal with Prevention of AIDS through sex education in schools at the secondary and senior secondary level in the light of social norms.

Types of LACs

There may be two types of local advisory committees *viz;* (a) Short Term Local Advisory Committees (*i.e.*, specific problem solving committees), and (b) Long Term Local Advisory Committees.

Short Term Local Advisory Committees are commonly found in most affluent countries. This type of committee is established to assist in solving immediate and short Term problems, such as AIDS awareness through meaningful sex education among adolescents. It term is usually of two to six months. Some educators believe that this type of committee is most effective and productive, since its members are given specific responsibilities for a limited period of time.

Long Term Advisory Local Committees are appointed for a period of 2-3 years to assist the Department of School Education in planning and carrying out sex education programmes. These programmes are undertaken to produce well educated citizens who will, after leaving schools, help in devising problem solving educational programmes to avoid frustration among high school students. These committees would prove effective because of their deeper understanding of the problems of schools especially related to prevention of AIDS in social structures.

Organization of LACs

Regarding organisation and power structures of the local advisory committees, the following information is desirable:

- Procedure for selection of the local advisory committee.
- Membership (rules and regulations).
- Frequency and minutes of the meetings.
- Implementation of the recommendations on the findings of the committee by the Department of Education; and
- Evaluation of the impact of the committee.

Selection of the LAC Members.

(i) Appointment by the Department of Education.
(ii) Selection by the Panchayat (Village Council)
(iii) Selection by community organisation represented on the committee, and
(iv) A combination of the above.

The selection of the committee members has to be made in different ways but should aim at a true representation of the local community keenly interested in a specific school problem such as prevention of AIDS among high school pupils through an effective programmes of meaningful sex education in schools at the secondary and senior secondary level.

Equal opportunities should be provided, as far as possible, to all community members irrespective of religion, caste, creed, political and economic considerations, although in some Asian countries this will present enormous problems in the foreseeable future due to diversity and size of the country. Liaison between these committees and the Department of Education should be deliberate, even obtrusive, to make their membership prestigious and accord them an official or at least a semi-official status.

Committee's Membership

It may indeed prove an extremely difficult task to form rural committees which are truly representative of the community. The effectiveness of a committee depends on the quality of services rendered by its members. It is true that individuals from the lower income section may not actively participate in the local advisory committees. There is a likelihood that those nominated to the committee will not truly represent the community. They are required to express the views of the community on educational problems and not their own opinions or those of the organizations to which they belong. The young as well as the old should have representation on the committee. Teachers will inevitably be involved in it, but they need not outnumber the non-teacher members. The Principal/Headmaster and District Education Officer should be *ex-officio* members of the committee without the right to vote.

Qualifications for LAC Members

(1) Civil servants with sound educational philosophy;
(2) Retired teachers;
(3) Professionals;
(4) High School teachers, and
(5) Persons interested in educational problems, issues especially those concerning high school AIDS prevention educational programmes through sex

education with leadership qualities and traits besides a good reputation in the community.

Selection of Officials

A local advisory committee should select its Chairman, Vice-Chairman and Secretary. The Chairman should preferably be a non-professional with a good reputation in the community, one who can feel the pulse of the community better.

Suggestions

1. The local advisory committee should be aware of local as well as national interests, while making any decision regarding transaction of sex education in schools.
2. The resource group should have a thorough knowledge of the local environment, needs, problems and economic conditions and resistance which may be exerted.
3. It should demonstrate the requisite competence in providing rural leadership communities;
4. It should have the ability to work with individuals and organisation with diametrically opposite views in a generally democratic and cooperative manner; and
5. There should be clear methods of communication. Any suggestion for prevention of AIDS through fostering healthy life style among students should be unanimously acceptable

Reverting to the specific AIDS Prevention through Sex Education, the following suggestions may be helpful:

To implement the AIDS preventive education programme through sex education and to involve teachers in the advisory committee, it may be imperative to orient the teacher through in-service and pre-service programmes. Orientation programmes may also be organized for teacher educators. The proposal to educate the teaching community about the role of advisory committees, their organization and functions is neither fanciful nor premature. Also, the programmes for the pre-service teachers would prove unrealistic, if the teacher educators remain ignorant about schools elsewhere in the country. Furthermore, teaching community should be aware of the techniques concerning counselling for AIDS.

Conclusion

It was pointed out in various national dailies that Asia might have most of the AIDS patients by the turn of century (2000AD). To overcome the AIDS monster, the Continent as a whole, *i.e.*, community members, social scientists, media professionals, medical professionals, teachers, and policy-makers were required to join hands in educating the persons regarding prevention of AIDS as there was no cure and vaccine for this killer disease. The only hope is prevention, which is through education. Coming to the specific of adolescents, especially in the school system, preventive educational AIDS programmes have to be initiated catering to the psycho-educational needs of our adolescents with reference to sex related concepts in the school curriculum especially at the secondary stage. Thus we need well qualified and understanding teachers who may establish compatible relationships with adolescents, their parents and the community. The author believes that AIDS prevention strategies discussed in this book are incomplete without the dedication and sincere interest on the part of the teacher. The teacher is the ultimate person who determines the outcome – no matter what is put in print regarding the educational endeavour. Teaching and learning strategies are tools. As teachers, administrators and lay-members of school management, we are forced by circumstances to face the menace of AIDS/HIV infection which has been with us since

1986. We cannot ignore this menace as it is going to affect our continent may be with horrible consequences. Finally, the community as a whole must be a part of preventive educational programmes concerning AIDS especially with adolescents. Thus to combat the AIDS menace in the school system, political and social leaders, educationists, textbook writers, media personnel and interested parents should work in unison and harmony.

To conclude, let us think, organize and strive together as a professional and concerned human beings to prevent this menace of AIDS/HIV infection among the adolescents through meaningful sex education in schools keeping in view the social, moral, ethical and cultural values.

Meaningful Healthy Life Style Education to the Adolescents

Guidelines for Teachers

The following are some suggestions which are neither meant to be prescriptive nor necessarily applicable in all the situations.

1. Compatible Relationships with Students

In order to impart meaningful sex education to our adolescents, teachers should form compatible relationship with students in order to illustrate positive attitude towards sex education. Teacher should be sensitive, sincere and able to build rapport with the students. Interesting facts lie behind the statistics. One, for example, is the students' most universal definition of what makes a good teacher.

> *"He's young .... has a sense of humour ... listens and understands ..... doesn't just go by the book ..... encourages discussion and participation ..... treats us like grown ups .... gives us responsibility always listens and is free and open with us .... is interested in us and thinks like a kind".*

2. Teacher as a Guide

Teacher should not impose his values on the students regarding sex related matters but act as a guide. In order to achieve the same, the teacher may develop the following skills.

(i) Patient hearing
(ii) Development of a scientific temperament
(iii) Suggesting by reasoning concept
(iv) Guiding
(v) Counselling

(i) Patient Hearing

This action calls for the following:

(a) the situation has to be understood ; or
(b) the problem pupils get annoyed by communicating in angry mood, the teacher must develop a skill to gain their confidence. The method of understanding the immature personality patterns of these adolescents is to encourage them towards logical reasoning and decision making.

(ii) Development of Scientific Temper

Inculcation of scientific temperament is confined often to the cultivation of an attitude of mere questioning process. The major components of the scientific temperament include: objective observation, experimentation, analyzing each point of view relevant to the inquiry in a logical manner till the emergence of truth through a process of verification. Thus, a teacher may develop such temperament in himself especially with adolescents while discussing sex related issues with them.

(iii) Suggesting by Reasoning

Suggesting is nothing but infusing matured ideas in other persons without a specific course of action. It happens in situations where there are various approaches to solve a problem especially in case of sex related issues. Role playing is an effective strategy in mastering this skill besides other teaching aids such as films or recorded arguments, where suggesting by reasoning is possible. Sometimes, this skill is quite effective in dealing with adolescents during deliberations on sex related matters.

(iv) Guiding

This is possible where voluntary help is sought. The teacher has to be quite knowledgeable about the problem in order to provide valuable guidance. Role playing is effective in schools, where sex related issues are frequently discussed openly in a class. Roles of the school adolescents seeking advice under various situations and the parents seeking similar advice can be played by the teacher or the school authorities.

(v) Counselling

Counselling may be divided into two categories : (i) Group Activity, and (ii) Individual Activity. It is combination of the skills of suggestion and guidance in a variety of situations. It may be developed through role playing for effective counselling.

3. Some Practical Strategies — transaction of sex education instructional material (Do's and Dont's) in the actual class-room situation.

Dont's

(i) Do not preach, do not impose your values, and do not degrade others' values.
(ii) Do not discourage questions from the students regarding sex related issues even if they are not very meaningful.

(iii) Do not evade answers to the questions if you are unable to answer the questions.
(iv) Do not interfere in the personal matters of the students.
(v) Do not stress that all the students should participate in values clarification strategies or answer questions related to sex education matters.
(vi) Do not discuss the students' comments regarding sex matters after the class.

Do's

(i) Respect students from different religious, socio-economic and cultural backgrounds.
(ii) Have confidence in the competence of adolescent students, their parents and the community members.
(iii) Show willingness and enthusiasm in teaching this subject.
(iv) Always give suggestions or ideas as your personal convictions.
(v) Emphasise the importance of sex education in daily life.
(vi) Discuss the relationship between love and sex. Love may be interpreted as the communication of one's deep involvement in the welfare of others.
(vii) The purpose of sex education in schools may be explained in the following manner :
   - To give correct biological information
   - To reduce fear of sex.
   - To put sex in a positive light and try to upgrade moral standards.

4. Sex Education – Responsibility of each and every School Teacher

Imparting instructions in sex education should be the responsibility of each and every teacher. It is a common practice and belief that sex education should be the domain of only the Biology teacher. Sex education does not simply deal with reproduction system but it goes beyond to touch social, cultural and humane aspects of students' life. Thus, involvement of teachers of social studies, language, science (Biology), physical education and other teachers is quite necessary in a programme of sex education.

5. Integrated Approach to Teaching and Learning Situation in Sex Education

Sex related instructional material should be incorporated and correlated with all secondary school subjects as far as possible. Correlation may be spontaneous. It is felt that a separate subject in sex education may increase curriculum load. Thus, in the first instance, it is suggested to have correlation of sex education material with secondary school curriculum subjects.

Conclusion

No matter what is put in print to ensure that a given sex education curriculum will be executed in such a way as to de-emphasize straight memorization of reproduction, biological facts and emphasize understanding the context of real problems. If the teacher does not sympathize with this approach or understands it, the programme of sex education or life skills or Adolescent Education will be not a meaningful venture. The most important contribution of the teacher must always be his ability to make interpretations, innovations, invent his own study units and make them come to life by adapting to opportunities in his classroom and living environment. He must be inventive in demonstrating examples of an idea from the resources at hand in specific situations.

Annexure - I

Policy Decisions on Health Education in Schools

Education Commission (1964–66)*

Education Commission (1964–66) popularly known as the Kothari Commission, after the name of its Chairman Professor D. K. Kothari, Chairman, University Grants Commission was the first Commission Independent India to examine the entire system of education at all levels and in all respects and to suggest reforms. Shri J. P. Naik, Head of the Department of Educational Planning, Administration and Finance, Gokhale Institute of Politics and Economics, Pune was its Member Secretary.

The Commission visited Universities, Colleges and Schools and held discussions with teachers, educationists, administrators and students. It interviewed nearly 9,000 men and women distinguished in public life, scientists, industrialists and scholars in different fields and others interested in education. It consulted a number of internationally well-known educationalists and scientists.

Recommendations of the Education Commission : Health Education and School Education

The Commission recommended the inclusion of 'Health Education' as a compulsory subject at the lower Primary Stage (Classes I to IV).

---

* **Source** : Secondary Education Commission Report (1964–66)

Health Education at Higher Education Stage

We recommend that early steps should be taken to organize adequate health services in universities and colleges. Health centres should be established on every university campus and in townships with a large student population to provide for medical examination, follow-up treatment, and emergency care. The services of part-time doctors should be enlisted for the purpose in smaller mofussil towns. We also recommend that adequate provision should be made for health education of students and for securing their involvement in the organization of health services — both in policy-making and in the execution of programmes. The UGC may explore the possibility of organizing health services for university teachers and students on the lines of the contributory health service organized for the employees of the Government of India. A beginning may be made with one or two universities with a large resident student population and, in the light of the experience gained, the programme may be extended to other centres.

National Policy on Education (1986 and as Modified in 1992)

The National policy on Education (NPE) formulated by the Government of India, Ministry of Education in 1986 and slightly modified in 1992 points out the directions of initiatives in the field of education. The NEP was prepared after the nation-wide debate. A Programme of Action to implement the directions contained in the NEP is being followed. It may also be observed that the thrust now in on human resource development and accordingly the erstwhile Ministry of Education's nomenclature was changed into Ministry of Human Resource Development, in the wake of the NPE

Health Education in NPE

Health Planning and health service management should optimally interlock with the education and training of appropriate categories of health manpower through health-related vocational courses. Health education at the primary and middle levels will ensure the commitment of the individual, to family and community health, and lead to health-related vocational courses at the +2 stage of higher secondary education. Efforts will be made to devise similar vocational courses based on Agriculture, Marketing, Social Services, etc. An emphasis in vocational education will also be on development of attitudes, knowledge, and skills for entrepreneurship and self-employment.

Yoga

As a system which promotes an integrated development of body and mind, yoga will receive special attention. Efforts will be made to introduce yoga in all schools. To this end, it will be introduced in teacher training courses.

(Note : This direction was incorporated in the revised NPE, 1992)

National Curriculum Framework in School Education (2000)*

In report to NPE, 1986 the National Curriculum for Elementary and Secondary Education: A Framework, 1988 was developed by the National Council of Educational Research and Training, New Delhi. It was put into practice. Since the curriculum development is not a one-time venture but an on-going process that was to be sensitive and

* **Source** : NCERT Curriculum + NPE documents (1992)

responsive to the changing needs, it was revised by the NCERT in 1999 and circulated in 2000 the revised curriculum all the subjects.

National Curriculum Framework for School Education on Health Education

Art of Healthy and Productive Living—Primary Stage

The need for introducing an interdisciplinary area of learning integrating the major concerns of Health and Physical Education, Art Education and Work Education has assumed greater significance. Despite clear allocation for time for these components in the earlier curriculum documents, little attention in reality has been paid to these. There have been logistic, conceptual and other difficulties experienced by the teachers and implementing agencies which contribute enormously towards the all-round development of the personality of children. The system seems to have experienced difficulties to be responsive to the developmental needs of the children. Another major factor leading to the half-hearted implementation of these areas could be lack of availability of proper motivation and evaluation procedures among teachers. Yet another bottleneck seems to be their presentation in a fragmented manner. As such, the proposed subject under the title 'Art of Healthy and Productive Living' is being recommended initially for primary classes which can be subsequently extended to upper primary classes.

The main objective of art of healthy and productive living is to develop aesthetic sensibilities and skills of healthful living besides providing a nurturing ground for love for labour, positive social attitudes and moral values so as to enable the child to be receptive to ideas of others with humility and sincerity in thought, word and deed. This will provide children with opportunities for their development into social human beings and dedicated and contributed citizens for the society and the nation. Love for mankind and helping the needy would germinate at this stage and its culmination would be in terms of attainment of selfless service-Seva.

Classes I and II

Experience such as scribbling, enjoying movements of the parts of body, deriving pleasure through seeing colour, figures and toys gained earlier would be strengthened. Children's natural urge to play out to be satisfied. The activities could be organised which help children make subjective choices about music and also drawing and painting in some shapes, developing clay models during play, and participating in group activities involving light exercises, group songs, theatrical arts and dances and imitative actions.

Teachers will have to develop activities keeping in mind local environment, cultural background of children and available resources. Teachers have to provide opportunities for free play and free expression to children with a focus on the objectives of each purposeful activity organised for them. It should be ensured that each child participates and learns certain good habits in practical sense. This stage is apt for value inculcation through story telling and dramatisation suiting to the level of maturity and understanding of learners. All such activities need to be presented in an integrated manner.

At this stage children may also develop a habit of keen observation and accurate description of things around them. They may pick up the skills of both, cleaning the teeth and dressing up. Now the children have also to learn behaviour and speech in formal settings. They are to be taught how to sit and stand properly and how to talk in a formal manner.

Classes III – V

At this stage, children develop better muscular coordination and acquire sensory discrimination. They develop a feeling of self and acquire the capability of knowing about themselves and the immediate environment surrounding them. The play at this stage may include light physical exercise and drill which can be combined with music. This is the stage when children can be taught to develop elementary knowledge relating to health, strength and beauty of the body. They may also develop the art of relaxation. Children should be initiated into the art of using and controlling senses related to hunger and thirst and regulating calls of nature. Their speech, behaviour, movement and action can be properly controlled. They may appreciate beauty in the objects around them and undertake exercises, and develop sense of preference for things and music. At this stage, attitude formation with regard to proper and healthy living in terms of cleanliness of body, surroundings, dress and place of sitting and eating, may be encouraged. Children at will also start liking activities pertaining to games and sports and would be introduced to the basic physical postures leading to yogic exercises. Mimicry and using various musical instruments will become part of their experience. Feeling of affection, friendship and social cohesion will be nurtured. Activities pertaining to drawing and painting, collage, clay modeling, printing, using masks, puppets and toys, folk dance, rangoli, alpana and the like may constitute the syllabi at this stage.

It will be desirable to orient teachers in undertaking activities pertaining to the art of healthy and productive living in an integrated manner. Suitable instructional materials both in print and non-print form including wall posters addressed to the teachers may prove to be of great help in initiating children to the art of healthy and productive living.

Health and Physical Education at the Middle and Secondary Stages (Class VI to X)

Health and physical education has to be concerned with total health of the learner and the community. It will include mental and emotional health besides physical health of the learners. The main aim of health and physical education programme should be to develop desirable understanding, attitude and practices with regard to nutrition, health and sanitation so as to improve health status of the self, family and the community. Learners need to be helped to develop an awareness about the health and sanitation at the community level and their role in that context. Physical education has to concentrate on developing health, strength and fitness of the body.

Games and sports have to find a prominent place in the total scheme of things. Emphasis should be on acquisition of adequate neuro-muscular coordination commensurate with their developmental stage. Yoga and meditation can be very well-organised under the regular school schedule to help children acquire concentration and relaxation.

Other important activities concerning the area of health and physical education include Scouting and Guiding, NCC, and Red-Cross which can help in cultivation of such basic qualities as endurance, courage, decision-making, resourcefulness, respect for others, truthfulness, faithfulness, loyalty to duty, and concern for the common good. Students' involvement in these activities would constructively channelise their energies and also promote and integrate learning in different curricular areas directly or indirectly. This would promote the latent curriculum of an institution.

With a view to promoting healthful living and solving major health problems of the country, the general education of first ten years must help develop a system which promotes an integral development of body, mind and spirit. Medical inspection and check-up should be compulsory at all the stages with adequate follow up in cases in which deficiencies are noticed. Health and physical education including games and sports should be considered an integral part of the learning process and be included in the evaluation of performance,

At upper primary stage keeping in view the characteristic physical growth, neuro-muscular coordination and social development, the learners may be exposed to vigorous developmental and rhythmic exercises, gymnastics, athletics, aquatics, judo, yoga, drill and marching, scouting and guiding camping and various team games and competitions. These options may be made available subject to the facilities available and the learners preferences. In health education, provision should be made for creation among learners an awareness related to common health problems, safety measures, nutritional problems, adulteration, first-aid, sanitation and pollution. Exercises of breath and yoga should receive special attention.

With regard to physical, mental and emotional health of learners, the secondary stage of education is particularly crucial. Rapid acceleration of growth and changes in appearance and functions of the body associated with the onset of puberty indicate the need of provision of appropriate guidance and counselling that would facilitate the adjustment and growth of children. Interests during this period narrow down to fewer games. The learner is likely to be more adventurous comparatively. Physical education should include more vigorous activities of various sorts including athletics, major games including indigenous games, gymnastics, yogic exercises, meditation, combatives, judo and swimming. The NCC, scouting and guiding and social service should be encouraged in addition to the compulsory programmes of physical education. In Classes IX and X, health education should enable the students to learn, in comparatively great detail, about personal health, impact of environmental pollution on health, food and nutrition, control and prevention of diseases, first aid, home nursing, and safety measures.

The knowledge of and activities related to personal and community health assume great importance. An awareness of HIV and AIDS may be given. Students may also be acquainted with evils associated with promiscuity and child and drug abuse. Adolescence education and sex-education may also be provided in a suitable manner. It would be desirable to generate suitable self-instructional material in this regard for different age groups of learners addressing to their needs and requirements and watching to the level of growth and maturity. It should be provided to all learners. Provision for separate teacher and classes may need not be encouraged. The whole approach should be such that the learner participates and learns ways of healhful living.

Rationale

Health is defined as "a state of physical, mental and social well-being and not merely the absence of disease or infirmity", (WHO) thus, it assumes great importance in the all-round development of a child. Health and Physical Education enable the pupil to attain such a state of health, in fact, becomes education for man.

A rational syllabus of health and Physical Education in school must, therefore, enable the pupil to know and understand that harmonious development of body and mind is essential for good health and it should help the pupil to raise his own health status. The syllabus should also be such that, if transacted effectively, it enables the pupil to contribute meaningfully, in order to raise the health status of the self, family, community and also of the environment to which he belongs.

In the National Curriculum Framework for School Education (2000), it has been emphasized that Health and Physical Education has to be concerned with total health of the learner and the community. It will include mental and emotional health besides physical health of the learners. The main aim of Health and Physical Education programme should be to develop desirably understanding, attitude and practices with regard to nutrition, health and sanitation so as to improve health status of the self, family and the community. Learners need to be helped to develop an awareness about the health and sanitation at the community level and their role in that context. Physical education has to concentrate on developing health, strength and fitness of the body. The National Policy on Education (1986) visualizes that Health and Physical Education should aim at enabling the child to know that harmonious development of body and mind is essential for good health. Physical, education should thus, aim at developing health, strength and fitness of the body along with emotional and social development

While some general principles of syllabus formulation in Health and Physical Education can be derived from the general theory of curriculum development, some specific considerations, to be taken into account will depend upon the nature of the subject and its relative importance in the entire curriculum framework. Some specific points which should be given proper thought while formulating the syllabus in this area for Classes VI to VIII are given below:

- The term 'Health and Physical Education' includes knowledge of health, science and physical activities including games, sports, and other recreational activities.
- All the programmes of Health and Physical Education are for all students. It should be incumbent on each and every student to participate in these programmes. The organization of any such programme at the upper Primary Stage should, therefore, ensure general participation by all and this should get preference over competition.
- The activities prescribed in the syllabus should cover a very wide range so that each and every pupil can participate according to her/his interest and needs, specially in physical activities.
- Activities which do not involve much cost or no cost activities may be identified because most schools cannot afford high cost apparatus.
- Facilities for physical education should be increasingly developed in rural as well as in urban schools. In this regard, special attention should be paid to socially and economically under-developed areas, urban slums, remote/rural and tribal areas.
- Content in health education syllabus should be meaningfully related to the pupil's environment and life.

Health and Physical Education at the Secondary Stage (Class IX, X)*

Health and Physical Education is concerned with the total health of the learner and the community. Besides physical health, it includes mental and emotional health of the learners. WHO defines health as "a state of physical, mental and social well-being and not merely the absence of disease or infirmity". The aim of Health and Physical Education is to enable the student to attain such a state of health, that it becomes an education for the total human being.

An effective syllabus of Health and Physical Education in school must, therefore, enable the learner to develop desirable understanding, attitude and practices with regard to nutrition, health and sanitation so as to improve health status of the self, family and the community and also of the environment to which she/he belongs and more importantly, the learner enters adulthood as a healthy person. Learners need to be helped to develop awareness about the health and sanitation at the community level and also their roles in that context. Physical education has to concentrate on developing health, strength and fitness of the body. National Policy on Education, 1986 and the subsequent curriculum frameworks of 1986 and 2000 have emphasized on this vital area of school education.

In this-respect, it is a truism to say that the practice of healthy living will serve as the foundation for physical education. It is envisaged that any effort to promote aesthetic values at the school level will include a natural esteem for physical well-being. The mastery of the body, its powers and qualities, requires knowledge, methodical

* **Source** : NCERT Curriculum Guidelines for Health & Physical Education

training and exercise. The body of the youth must be ^strengthened, its skills and capacities developed, the muscles and nerves trained, the senses cultivated and hygienic and proper dietary habits inculcated. Therefore, provision has to be made much more systematically than before, in the school curriculum for Health and Physical Education. At the Secondary level acquisition of / the habits of healthy living and participation in games and sports and athletics for the neuro muscular coordination and physical fitness are the aims which should be taken care of while developing any syllabus of Health and Physical Education.

While developing the syllabus in Health and Physical Education some of the specific considerations kept in view for the secondary stage of education are as follows :

- The term Health and Physical Education includes knowledge of Health Science and more vigorous activities of various sorts including athletics, major games including indigenous games. gymnastics, yogic exercises, meditation, combative, judo and swimming. The NCC, NSS, scouting and guiding and social service should also be encouraged in addition to the compulsory programmes of physical education.
- All programmes of Health and Physical Education are for all students. As such it should be ensured that all students participate in these programmes. At the same time an element of healthy competition should also be cautiously introduced.
- The activities prescribed in the syllabus - should be of wide-range so that each and every pupil can participate according to his/her interest and needs, specially in physical activities.

- Activities Involving no cost or low cost may be identified so that most of the schools can implement the programmes easily.
- Facilities for Physical Education should be increasingly developed In rural as well as urban schools. In this regard, special attention should be paid to socially and economically under-developed areas, urban slums, rural, tribal and remote areas.
- The content in Health and Physical Education syllabus should be useful and appropriate to the pupil's environment and life. Duplication of topics between health and science education may be avoided.
- The syllabus in Physical Education should be such that talent in sports and games is discovered. In classes IX and X, there should be provision for training/ coaching for talented students. This will help to catch them young. This training/ coaching may be intensified for promising students.

Objectives

- To bring the overall awareness of values and to inculcate among students the desired habits and attitudes towards health and to raise their health status;
- To make the pupils physically, mentally and emotionally fit and to develop their personal and social qualities that will help them to be good human beings;
- To develop a scientific point of view regarding health and physical education;
- To identify personal, family and community health problems and acquire relevant scientific knowledge and information to prevent and control these problems to stay healthy;
- To take action, individually and collectively to protect and promote (i) their own health; and (ii) health of

their family members; (iii) health of those around them in the community, seeking help when required from available community resources;

- To promote improved preventive and promotive self-care behaviour in the families and in the community;
- To develop awareness of HIV, AIDS and drug abuse in the community;
- To develop an awareness regarding the importance of physical fitness and organic efficiency in individual and social life;
- To develop awareness regarding transfer of fundamental processes to physical activities of one's choice;
- To develop interest in exercise, sports and games for self-satisfaction and making it a part of life;
- To enable an individual to enhance inner qualities as self-mastery, discipline, courage, confidence and efficiency;
- To enable an individual to display a sense of responsibility, patriotism, self-sacrifice and service to the community in a better way;
- To develop awareness of the importance of self-defence and self-dependence;
- To develop awareness of good posture so that one may strive to maintain a good posture;
- To enable an individual to lead an enthusiastic and active life;
- To enable an individual to practise socially acceptable behavioural patterns in an impressive manner.

Learning Outcomes

The syllabus in Health and Physical Education at this stage aims at realizing the following learning outcomes:

Learning Outcomes in Health Education

- The learners develop a scientific point of view of health and physical education;
- They identify personal, family and community health problems and are able to prevent and control these problems to stay healthy;
- They take action individually and collectively to protect and promote their own health, health of their family and of the people around them in the community;
- They are always ready to promote improved preventive and promotive self-care behaviour in the family and in the community.

Learning Outcome in Physical Education

- The learners -develop organic fitness, normal sense organs and efficient organic systems;
- They cultivate habits of engaging in appropriate exercises so that immediate and future health needs will be met;
- They develop neuro-muscular skills that promote the ability to perform work with ease and grace;
- They develop attitudes of cooperation, good sportsmanship and fair-play;
- They cultivate such traits of character as self-mastery, discipline, courage and confidence:
- They develop a sense of patriotism, self-reliance, self-sacrifice and a desire to serve;
- They prepare themselves for making a worthy use of leisure time by acquiring knowledge of sports for the purpose of participation or observing, appreciating and enjoying them.

Content

For realizing the above mentioned learning outcomes, suitable content is to be included in the syllabus. As such this syllabus should be well-planned and broad-based. The content has to be properly graded on the basis of each age-group. It should also maintain continuity from one stage or class to the other and ensure progressive capacities in students that will prove challenging to them. The following list of contents, which is only suggestive, can be considered for inclusion in the syllabus of Health and Physical Education.

Health Education

- Meaning and Nature of Health;
- Environment and Health;
- Major accidents, which can be fatal in rural and urban areas. First Aid;
- Nutrition;
- Health hazards of modernization; Drug Abuse, HIV and AIDS;
- Communicable and non-communicable diseases. Approved systems of medicine being practised in our country;
- Importance of lnternational Health.

Physical Education

- Dance
- Sports and Games (including training/ coaching)
- Yoga
- Athletics
- Gymnastics
- Swimming
- Combative

Physical Education activities are dependent upon the facilities available in and around the school. Therefore, the teacher should develop programmes taking into consideration the facilities available in the school and in the community.

Methodology

Though some topics of Health Education can be taught in the class by using traditional methods, sometimes team-teaching becomes necessary as the Health Education component is integrated in other subjects like Work Education, Environmental Studies, Sciences and Languages, etc.

Physical Education and activities of Health Education also cannot be taught in isolation. Rather, it is done in such a way that students actively participate and imbibe positive attitudes. It is essential, for its successful transaction, to develop plans of action well before the academic session starts and assess the responsibility so that the package of activities is carried out in a logical sequence. In this, the cooperation of other staff-members often becomes essential, which may be ensured by the Physical Education teacher.

Evaluation

Evaluation in Health and Physical Education should be based upon the student's individual capacity, performance and progress. Assessment should, therefore, be continuous and comprehensive using rating scale, check list and observation and should be such as to measure the multidimensional progress of the student.

Annexure - II

India's Recent Programmes to Fight Against HIV/AIDS*

Prevention of HIV/AIDS : A Trepartite Response

'...A healthy workforce is the biggest asset for the company .....A healthy workforce would mean less of absenteeism that translates into better productivity..', says Mr. Madhur Bajaj, Vice Chairman, Bajaj Auto Limited in the ILO kit "Enterprises and HTV/AIDS in India."

The ILO India under its project "Prevention of HIV/ AIDS in the world of work: A Tripartite Response", documented the HTV/AIDS experiences of eight leading private and public sector enterprises. Health of workers and its link to production is one of the main reasons why enterprises have chosen to respond to HIV/AIDS in India. The project is trying to share the experiences of these companies with others and providing them technical assistance to help them develop their policy and programmes on HIV/AIDS.

The project has selected the states of West Bengal, Madhya Pradesh and Jharkhand for strengthening the world of work response. Building enterprises-based interventions is the key focus in these states. From January 2003 to March 2004, the interventions were initiated in 55 companies, which together reach more than 100,000 workers. The key to the

* Source : NACO

ILO approach is that ILO funds none of these enterprises. The ILO only provides them technical support in terms of training of master trainers/peer educators and IEC materials. 628 trainers have been trained in these enterprises, who are from different units within the enterprises like the management, welfare, trade unions, occupational safety and health etc. "The whole idea is to institutionalize HIV/AIDS interventions within the companies for the sake of sustainability", says S. Mohd. Afsar, the National Project Coordinator, ILO Project.

Apart from building enterprise-based interventions, the project also collaborates with the trade unions, employers' organizations and Ministry of Labour. Trade unions are getting involved and seeing the importance of HIV/AIDS programmes for protecting rights and health of workers.

The project is making efforts to develop a non-discriminatory policy at workplace using the ILO Code of Practice on HIV/AIDS and the world of work. The NACO has already encouraged adoption of the ILO code at workplaces. The ILO, with National Labour Institute and Indian Network for People Living with HIV/AIDS (PLWHA) organized a national level workshop to reduce HIV related stigma and discrimination in the world of work. ILO in New Delhi, along with Lawyers collective, organised a consultantion on the draft legislation on HIV/AIDS with world of Work partners in December 2003.

Access to Treatment for People Living With HIV/AIDS

WHO and UNAIDS have launched a global initiative called "3 by 5" with the objective of providing antiretroviral therapy (ART) to 3 million people living with HIV/AIDS in developing countries by the end of 2005. This global WHO/

UNAIDS initiative coincides with the Government of India's announcement on the eve of World AIDS Day 2003 to provide Anti-retrovial treatment free of cost to 100,000 people living with HIV/ AIDS by end 2005 starting April 1, 2004. At the initial stage free ARV will be provided in the six high prevalence states to children below 15 years, mothers under the "Prevention of Parent To Child Transmission" (PPCTC) programme and people with AIDS who access government hospitals.

The Indian government has until now actively supported the care and support of people living with HIV/ AIDS by - among other things - provisioning drugs for management of opportunistic infections and providing antiretrovirals in the PPCTC programmes cosponsored by UNICEF. Antiretroviral treatment has, however, not been available to people living with HTV/AIDS except for those who were able to pay the high costs themselves and in some selected government schemes.

Making ART available to people living with HIV/AIDS (PLWHAs) is critical to ensuring the health and well-being of PLWHAs. However, the roll out of ART is not easy. The critical challenges of provisioning and scaling up access to ART are many and therefore it calls for a comprehensive joint effort from all sectors involved in the response to HIV/AIDS - not only from the health care sector. The challenges are, among others:

- Mobilizing continued and sustainable political/ bureaucratic leadership and commitment
- Mobilizing adequate resource
- Strengthening capacity of the health system for ART delivery
- Ensuring a steady supply of anti-retroviral drugs and diagnostics

- Ensuring treatment adherence and community participation
- Strengthening of and linking up with entry points such as Voluntary Counseling and Testing Centres and PPTCT sites
- Improving the quality of care and laboratory services.
- Monitoring, evaluation, surveillance and research
- Developing communication strategies for enhancing community involvement

Theme Group's initiative

The UN Theme Group on HIV/ AIDS, consisting of the UN Co-sponsors, bilateral donors and the Indian Network for Positive People (INP+), is fully committed to the Global "3 by 5 initiative" and the Government of India's initiative to scale up ART treatment. They are actively supporting the rolling out of this pioneering initiative by the National AIDS Control Organisation. Commitments from the UN agencies have been in terms of capacity building, technical assistance and channeling of funds. WHO, UNAIDS and UNICEF have been contributing in organizing consultations, developing training materials and facilitating the training programmes.

Keeping in view the operational framework of the free ART initiative of the Government of India, the UN Theme Group on HIV/AIDS in line with the government initiative is planning a "Model Care System". The project is expected to provide valuable lessons and a demonstration effect for implementation of ART. The proposal is also expected to explore public-private partnerships as a strategy to ensure cost effective interventions and sustainability. Networks of people living with HIV/AIDS will be crucial allies and integral to the treatment initiative. The project is expected to be initiated soon, after assessing the situation in the four identified districts and strengthening the human and technical resources. This project will be integrated in the existing health infrastructure in the districts and be in concurrence with the NACO's ART operational guidelines and look at care in a comprehensive manner and not as a stand-alone ART programme. The envisaged districts are Bellary in Kamataka, Guntur in Andhra Pradesh, Sangli in Maharashtra and one district in Nagaland.

Anti-retroviral treatment (ART)

HIV/AIDS is not curable, but with ART it can be treated:

- ART prolongs lives, making HIV/AIDS a chronic disease, not a death sentence. Affluent countries have seen a 70% decline in HIV/AIDS deaths.
- ART will help calm fears and change attitudes towards HTV.
- ART, integrated with'prevention, can significantly reduce HIV transmission.
- ART, once very costly, is now much more affordable, safer and easier to use.
- ART can reduce overall health care costs to the family and community and restore quality of life for the individual.
- ART can be an incentive for people to get tested
- ART can return sick people back to productive lives

Annexure - III

Adult HIV Prevalance

Comparative Data of Countries*

Countries and terrotries	*(%) Adult HIV prevalence rate (15-49 years) 2001*	*Countries and terrotries*	*(%) Adult HIV prevalence rate (15-49 years) 2001*
Afghanistan	—	Bolivia	0.10
Albania	—	Bosnia and Herzegovina	<0.1
Algeria	0.1	Botswana	38.8
Andorra	—	Brazil	0.65
Angola	5.5	Brunei Darussalam	—
Antigua and Barbuda	—	Bulgaria	<0.1
Argentina	0.69	Burkina Faso	6.5
Armenia	0.15	Burundi	8.3
Australia	0.07	Cambodia	2.7
Austria	0.24	Cameroon	11.8
Azerbaijan	<0.1	Canada	0.31
Bahamas	3.5	Cape Verde	—
Bahrain	0.26	Central African Republic	12.9
Bangladesh	<0.1	Chad	3.6
Barbados	1.2	Chile	0.30
Belarus	0.27	China	0.11
Belgium	0.16	Colombia	0.40
Belize	2	Comoros	—
Benin	3.6	Congo	7.2
Bhutan	<0.1		

* **Source** : The State of World's Children 2003, UNICEF

Countries and terrotries	*(%) Adult HIV prevalence rate (15-49 years) 2001*	*Countries and terrotries*	*(%) Adult HIV prevalence rate (15-49 years) 2001*
Congo Democratic Republic of the	4.9	Greece	0.17
Cook Islands	—	Grenada	—
Costa Rica	0.55	Guatemala	1.0
Cote d'Ivoire	9.7	Guinea	—
Croatia	<0.1	Guinea-Bissau	2.8
Cuba	<0.1	Guyana	2.7
Cyprus	0.25	Haiti	6.1
Czech Republic	<0.1	Holy See	—
Danmark	0.15	Honduras	1.6
Djibouti	—	Hungary	0.06
Dominica	—	Iceland	0.15
Dominican Republic	2.5	India	0.79
East Timor	—	Indonesia	0.10
Ecuador	0.30	Iran (Islamic Republic of)	<0.1
Egypt	<0.1	Iraq	<0.1
El Salvador	0.60	Ireland	0.11
Equatorial Guinea	3.4	Israel	0.10
Eritrea	2.8	Italy	0.37
Estonia	1	Jamaica	1.2
Ethiopia	6.4	Japan	<0.1
Fiji	0.07	Jordan	<0.1
Finland	<0.1	Kazakhstan	0.07
France	0.33	Kenya	15
Gabon	—	Kiribati	—
Gambia	1.6	Korea, Democratic People's Republic of	—
Georgia	<0.1	Korea, Republic of	<0.1
Germany	0.10	Kuwait	—
Ghana	3		

Countries and terrotries	(%) Adult HIV prevalence rate (15-49 years) 2001	Countries and terrotries	(%) Adult HIV prevalence rate (15-49 years) 2001
Kyrgyzstan	<0.1	Myanmar	—
Lao People's Democratic Republic	<0.1	Mamibia	22.5
Latvia	0.40	Nauru	—
Lebanon	—	Nepal	0.49
Lesotho	31.0	Netherlands	0.21
Liberia	—	New Zealand	0.06
Libyan Arab Jamahiriya	0.24	Nicaragua	0.20
Liechtenstein	0.07	Niger	—
Lithuania	—	Nigeria	5.8
Luxembourg	0.16	Niue	—
Madagascar	0.29	Norway	0.08
Malawi	15.0	Occupied Palestinian Territory	—
Malaysia	0.35	Oman	0.11
Maldives	0.06	Pakistan	0.11
Mali	1.7	Palau	—
Malta	0.13	Panama	1.5
Marshall Islands	—	Papua New Guinea	0.65
Mauritania	—	Paraguay	—
Mauritius	0.10	Peru	0.35
Mexico	0.28	Philippines	<0.1
Micronesia (Federated States of)	—	Poland	0.1
Moldova, Republic of	0.24	Portugal	0.52
Monaco	—	Qatar	—
Mongolia	<0.1	Romania	<0.1
Morocco	0.08	Russian Federation	0.90
Mozambique	13.0	Rwanda	8.9
		Saint Kitts and Nevis	—
		Sant Lucia	—

Countries and terrotries	*(%) Adult HIV prevalence rate (15-49 years) 2001*
Saint Vincent and the Grenadines	—
Samoa	—
San Marino	—
Sao Tome and Principe	—
Saudi Arabia	—
Senegal	0.50
Seychelles	—
Sierra Leone	7.0
Singapore	0.20
Slovakia	<0.1
Slovenia	<0.1
Solomon islands	—
Somalia	1.0
South Africa	20.1
Spain	0.50
Sri Lanka	<0.1
Sudan	2.6
Suriname	1.2
Swaziland	33.4
Sweden	0.08
Switzerland	0.5
Syrian Arab Republic	—
Tajikistan	<0.1
Tanzania United Republic of	7.8
Thailand	1.8
The former Yugoslav Republic of Macedonid	<0.1
Togo	5.0
Tonga	—
Trinidad and Tobago	2.5
Tunisia	—
Turkey	<0.1
Turkmenistan	<0.1
Tuvalu	5.0
Uganda	1.0
Ukraine	—
United Arab Emirates	—

Regional Summaries

Countries and terrotries	*(%) Adult HIV prevalence rate (15-49 years) 2001*	*Countries and terrotries*	*(%) Adult HIV prevalence rate (15-49 years) 2001*
Sub-Saharan Africa	8.6	CEE/CIS and Baltic States	0.44
Middle East and North Africa	0.30	Industrialized countries	0.35
South Asia	0.63	Developing countries	1.3
East Asia and Pacific	0.19	Least developed countries	3.5
Latin America and Caribbean	0.63	World	1.2

Suggested Readings

Adam, Eleanor., (21 April 1967), "Sex Education : The Swedish System." Scholastic Teacher 90, no. 11 pp. 16-17.

Allan, Gary., 1969, Sex Education Problems. Betmonts, Mass. : American Opinion, c.. pp 30.

Atarov, T.S., 1964 " Sex Education." In Soviet Education, edited by Helen B. Redl, pp. 53-77. New York : Free Press.

Bach, J., 1965 "Health, Sex and Family Education." In UNESCO, Health Education, Sex Education and Education for Home and Family Life, pp. 53-54. Hamburg : UNESCO Institute of Education.

Bauer, W.W., 1963, Moving into Manhood: ; A Guide for the Adolescent. Garden City, N.Y.: Doubleday & Co.,. 107 pp.

Boethuys, C.G., 1989 Swedish Experience – An Historical Perspective in "The Other Curriculum – European Strategies for School Sex Education, editor Herdith, Philip, International Planned Parenthood Federation.

Bhardwaj (Trans), 1994, Light of Truth, (Swami Daya Nand Saraswati), SAPS Publishers, New Delhi.

Billy, John O.G. et al, "The Sexual Behaviour of Men in the United States", Family Planning Perspective, 25 (2), 50-82.

Blanton, Smiley M.D., 1966, Love or Perish, New York: Simon and Schusser, Inc..

Catholic World. (July 1965) "Sex and Youth: Pastoral Directives of the German Episcopats." Catholic World 201. Pp. 264-268.

Clemans, Martva. (January 1967) "Learning about Sex.," Trends in Education. No. 5, pp. 9-15.

Dawkinds, Julia. A Textbook of Sex education. Oxford: BaSIL Blockwell, 1967, 98 pp.

Ellis, Albert and Alkbert Abarbanel (ed.), "The Encyclopaedia of Sexual Behaviour", Volumes One and Two, New York: Hawthorne Books, Inc.

Faridi, F.L., 1899 "Hijras", J.M. Campbell (Compiler), Gazetteer of the Bombay Presidency, 4(1), Bombay: Government Central Press,.

Forman, I. (October 1969) "Sex and Family Living: Training Project at Boston University School of Education." American Education 5 pp.11-15.

Ganguli, H.C., 1988 Behavioural Research in Sexuality, Delhi: Vikash Publishing Housed Pvt. Ltd.

Kakkar, S., 1989 "Intimate Relations: Exploring Indian Sexuality", New Delhi, Penguin Books India Pvt. Ltd.,.

Kaiser Network (2003), "India must act to prevent tens of millions of HIV cases", Daily HIV/AIDS Report, July 25 UNAIDS.

Kalra, R.M., Drug Addiction in Schools, Sterling Publishers, New Delhi.

Kalra, R.M., 1966AIDS and Adolescent - A New Generation at Risk, Vikash Publishers, New Delhi.

Karein, Arno, 1971 "Sexuality and Homosexuality", New York: W.W., Norton & Co. ,.

Katralwe Lindahl, August, 1995 Sexuality Education from a Swedish Perspective for Sex Education (RFSU),.

Kumar, S. (2003), "HIV cases rising sharply in India", BMJ, August 2.

Lancester, J. (2003), "AIDS Begins to widen its reach in India", Washington Post, June 11.

Link, W.R., (December 1969) "Teacher's View of Sex Education." Independent School Bulletin 29, pp. 10-11. "Discussion," Vol. 29 (May 1970), pp. 43-44.

Manley, Halen. 1964 A Curriculum Guide in Sex Education. St. Louis, Mo. : State Publishing Co., 59 pp.

NACO (2003), "HIV/AIDS Surveillance in India", www.naco.nic.in.

Nag Moni, 1994 "Sexual Behaviour and AIDS in India", Altimore: John Hopkin Univ.,.

Neff, N. (May 1970) "Sex education in the Public Schools : An Opinion". School and Community 56, P. 20.

Sexology, 1990 Sexual Policy and Sex Education in Sweden (1920-199) 20th Anniversary Lecture Meeting, , The Japanese Association for Sex Education, Tokyo.

Steward E. Fraser (Ed), 1972 "Sex, School and Society, International Perspectives", London : Aurora Publishers, Inc..

Szaz, G. (March 1970) "Sex Education and the Teacher." Journal of School Health 40, pp. 150-155.

The Lancet (2003), "Spreading the word about HIV / AIDS in India", Vol. 361, May 3.

UNESCO Institute for Education. Health Education, Sex Education and Education for Home and Family Life. Report of a meeting. International Studies in Education, February 17-22, 1964, Hamburg: UNESCO Institute for Education, 1965. pp 118.

U. Choudhry (2003), "UN warns India is sitting on AIDS bomb as 4,58 million already infected", Agence France Presse, July 28.

Additional Relevant Readings (International)

EDUCDATION FOR SEXUALITY: CONCEPTS AND PROGRAMS FOR TEACHERS. 2nd edition,. John J. Burt and Linda Meets, New York : W.B. Saunders Op. 1975.

FAMILY EDUCATION : A PROBLEM SOLVING CURRICULUM FOR ADOLESCENT (AGES 15-19). Memphis. TN: Planned Parenthood of Memphis, 1980.

FAMILY LIFE EDUCATION: CURRICULUM. Revised edition. Streven Bignell, ed., Sants Crus. CA: Network Publications, 1980.

A GUIDEBOOK FOR TEACHING FAMILY LIVING. Lynne Despelder and Nathalie Prettyman. Boston: Allyn and Bacon, 1980.

MORAL DEVELOP : A GUIDE TO PIAGET AND KOHLBERT. Ronald Dusks and Marieellen Whean. New York: Paulist Press: 1975.

TEACHING MATERIALS AND STRATEGIES: IMPLEMENTATION OF FAMILY LIFE EDUCATION CURRICULUM. Joan Beneach, Jean Kapp;, Louise Pelguin. Washington, D.C. : Sex Education Coalition of Metropolitan Washington, 1980.

VALUES IN SEXUALITY : A NEW APPROACH TO SEX EDUCATION. Eleanor S. Morrison and Mila Underhill; New York : Hart Publishing Co., 1974.

Plant, M. (ed) AIDS, DRUGS AND PROSTITUTION, Routledge, London, 1990.